Girl Talk

Also by Carolyn Mahaney
Feminine Appeal

Carolyn Mahaney & Nicole Mahaney Whitacre

Girl Talk

Mother-Daughter Conversations on Biblical Womanhood

CROSSWAY BOOKS

A PUBLISHING MINISTRY OF
GOOD NEWS PUBLISHERS
WHEATON, ILLINOIS

Cover design: Josh Dennis

First printing 2005

Printed in the United States of America

Library of Congress Cataloging-in-Publication Data

Mahaney, Carolyn, 1955-

    Girl talk : mother-daughter conversations on biblical womanhood / Carolyn Mahaney and Nicole Mahaney Whitacre

        p. cm.

    Includes bibliographical references.

    ISBN 13: 978-1-58134-510-0

    ISBN 10: 1-58134-510-0 (tpb)

    1. Women—Religious aspects—Christianity. 2. Christian women—Religious life. 3. Mothers and daughters. I. Mahaney Whitacre, Nicole. II. Title.

BT704.M336   2005

248.8'43—dc22   2004029336

BP		16	15	14	13	12	11	10	09	08	07
15	14	13	12	11	10	9	8	7	6	5	4	3

To C. J.
"If ever two were one, then surely we;
If ever man were loved by wife, then thee."
Carolyn

To Steve
"As you are mine, I am yours.
I give away myself for you and dote upon the exchange."
Nicole

Contents

Acknowledgments   9

Introduction: The Shopping Trip   13

PART ONE
The Forging of the Mother-Daughter Bond

1   The Language of Biblical Womanhood   *Carolyn*   23

2   Imperfect Makes Perfect   *Nicole*   29

3   Cover Mom   *Nicole*   35

4   Afternoon Out   *Carolyn*   41

5   Constant Communication   *Carolyn*   49

6   Conflict Jungle   *Nicole*   57

7   A Mother's Faith   *Carolyn*   63

8   A Mother's Example   *Carolyn*   69

9   A Mother's Love   *Carolyn*   75

10   A Mother's Discipline   *Carolyn*   81

11   A Daughter's Honor   *Nicole*   87

12   A Daughter's Obedience   *Nicole*   93

PART TWO
Biblical Womanhood in the Real World

13   Sowing in Springtime   *Nicole*   101

14   It's a Girl!   *Carolyn*   105

15   Foolish Fans and the Fear of God   *Nicole*   113

16   Best Friends   *Nicole*   119

17   What About Guys?   *Nicole*   125

18   True Beauty   *Carolyn*   131

19   Taking God to the Gap   *Nicole*   137

20   Future Homemakers   *Nicole*   143

21   Homemaking Internship   *Carolyn*   149

22	A Girl's Reputation *Carolyn*	157
23	When It Comes to Courtship *Carolyn*	163
24	Who Gives This Woman? *Carolyn*	169
25	Passing on the Language of Biblical Womanhood *Carolyn & Nicole*	175

Appendix A: Girl Talk Discussion Questions   179

Appendix B: More Girl Talk Questions   195

Appendix C: How to Lead Your Daughter to Christ   197

Appendix D: Mother-Daughter Memories   203

Appendix E: A Modesty Heart Check   205

A Word to Fathers *by C. J. Mahaney*   209

Notes   217

Acknowledgments

CAROLYN AND NICOLE would like to wholeheartedly thank:

Lane and Ebeth Dennis for your ever-gracious support and for giving us the priceless opportunity to write a book together. Marvin Padgett for your vast reservoir of patience from which you answered all our questions, accommodated our many requests, and granted numerous deadline extensions. Lila Bishop for your proficient editing and your kindness in explaining to us the finer points of grammar. Josh Dennis for allowing two unartistic women to offer suggestions on the book's cover. Thanks for the dedicated effort and creativity you invested to come up with a design that would appeal to teenage girls.

Gary and Lisa Thomas, Janice Dillon, Nora Earles, Susan Nelson, Julie Kauflin, Megan Russell, Jennifer and Naomi Hinders, Susan Jansen, Jenny Detwiler, Janis Shank, Cheri Kittrell, Sarah Loftness, and Joshua Harris for your invaluable critiques, encouragement, and assistance to make *Girl Talk* a reality. This book bears the handprint of each one of you.

The pastors and members of Covenant Life Church and Sovereign Grace Church of Fairfax for your faithful prayers: We were carried by them. And special thanks to the pastors of Sovereign Grace Church for your generous financial gift when Nicole's ancient laptop expired halfway through the writing process.

Nicole would like to thank Alyssa Sieb, Heidi Farley, the pastors' wives of Sovereign Grace Church, and all her friends for the meals, prayers, baby-sitting, encouraging notes and e-mails, and for still being my friends even though I went AWOL to write this book!

Jeff Purswell and Randy Stinson for bringing your theological precision and expertise to bear on chapter 14.

Carolyn McCulley. As if you weren't busy enough writing your own book, you joyfully put up with our phone calls and e-mails asking for your advice on our book. Thanks for being a wise, faithful, and always-encouraging counselor throughout the duration of this project. "Just one more question . . ."

Justin Taylor, who is a hero in our eyes for agreeing to read and edit *Girl Talk*—not once, but twice! We are so humbled and honored to have been on the receiving end of your exceptional counsel and gifting for this project.

Kristin Chesemore and Janelle Bradshaw for making meals, baby-sitting, praying, and being our most faithful cheerleaders. Thanks especially for letting us tell stories about you, for discussing all aspects of *Girl Talk*, and for helping us talk about something else once in a while. This is your book too. (And to Brian and Mike for your faithful encouragement and participation in family book discussions.)

Nancy Whitacre, the undisputed MVP of this book project. Thanks for baby-sitting your grandson, Jack, doing Nicole's laundry, cooking meals, and generally keeping the household running. Thank you also for your specific, timely encouragement and for your helpful suggestions. (Nope, we're not adding another chapter!) Your behind-the-scenes sacrifice made *Girl Talk* possible. I am sure no daughter-in-law has ever had a finer mother-in-law. (And to Bill and Megan for joyfully releasing Nancy to serve Nicole. Steve, Nicole, and Jack love sharing a home with you all.)

Our sons, Chad and Jack, whom we love with all our hearts. We hope this book will serve the young girl who is destined to be your wife someday.

C. J./Dad for being our most enthusiastic supporter on the planet. As our in-house editor, you protected us from theological error, challenged points that didn't make sense, and patiently walked us through rigorous rewrites. Your exceptional leadership as a husband and father has been the foundation and catalyst for our mother-daughter relationships. There would be no *Girl Talk* apart from you.

Finally, Steve Whitacre. You are most worthy of honor for your selfless and yet ever-joyful commitment to this book. Thank you for coming up with the title, discovering the opening illustration, skillfully editing the entire manuscript ("Sticklers Unite!"), taking care of Jack on your days off, tenderly caring for an exhausted wife in the final days of writing, and most of all for not letting Nicole quit! No one sacrificed more or contributed more to *Girl Talk*.

Our prayer for this book echoes that of Philip Doddridge:

"However weak and contemptible this work may seem in the eyes of the children of this world, and however imperfect it really be, [may it] nevertheless live before thee; and through a divine power, be mighty to produce the rise and progress of religion."[1]

Introduction:
The ſhopping Trip

DEAR MOTHERS AND DAUGHTERS,

We're a little blurry-eyed this morning. We just returned last night from the Mahaney Girls' Shopping Trip—our annual twenty-four-hour excursion into the wilds of northern Virginia retail country.

Wish you coulda been there. But you'd be stained with fruit punch and hot chocolate by now. As usual, we had a couple of spills. All part of the fun. We stayed at a hotel, bought a pile of Christmas gifts, walked at least fifty miles, and laughed a lot. When we finally left the mall after dark, we drove around aimlessly for half an hour before going home. We didn't want it to end.

Best we can figure, this was our fifteenth year. On the inaugural trip, Nicole (the oldest) was an awkward twelve and Kristin a year younger. Carolyn (Mom) didn't have any gray hairs yet. Janelle (the youngest) came a few years later when Mom determined she was old enough—and then only for the food. Not much has changed!

Actually a lot has changed. All three girls have gotten married, and four grandsons have been added to the family (three of them are Kristin's; so we pray for her a lot!). But in spite of weddings and moves to other states (and back again) and emergency surgeries and busy ministry schedules (all the girls married aspiring pastors), the Shopping Trip has survived.

Each year we've shared countless fits of hysterical laughter (you had to be there) punctuated by serious and memorable discussions about God, life, our hearts. Of course there has been conflict and more than a few spills (this year we set a new record!). Although every Shopping Trip has its own unique memories (like the time Kristin left her wallet full of cash at the Gap), there are certain things you can count on. Like Nicole's and Kristin's perennial argument about how to organize the family gift-giving. "Should we give presents to each other or only to the grandsons?" "Should everyone give to everyone, or should we pick names?" "How much should we spend so it's fair?" Kristin always has a plan, and Nicole always disagrees. Janelle's happy either way, as long as we talk about it over lunch.

Nicole, the complicated one, usually arrives with a Christmas list to rival Saint Nicholas. She wants to buy "small" gifts for all the cousins (twenty-seven total), all the people she's ever worked with and their kids, and anyone she's ever said "hi" to at church. Because of budgetary limitations she solicits ideas for homemade projects that fit within her also-very-limited creative abilities. We try to help. So there was the hot-chocolate-mix year and the homemade-cookies year and finally the just-buy-everyone-a-cheap-CD year. Paring down her list takes some time. Meanwhile Janelle is getting hungry. She's ready to take a break, and we haven't even started shopping yet.

Taking a break is the furthest thing from Kristin's mind. She's armed with coupons, sales advertisements, and a Christmas list complete with dollar amounts (she's put money aside every month for the last year). She takes this shopping thing a little too seriously. We almost feel bad for the clerks. They don't stand a chance against her thorough research and polite assertiveness. It usually goes something like this:

> Kristin (to clerk): "Good morning, ma'am. I have a question. [Here it comes!] According to this coupon, these T-shirts should be three for fifteen dollars, but they are marked seven dollars each."

Clerk (confidently): "Ah, yes, well, that sale ended last week."

Kristin (very sweetly): "Oh, I see. But may I point out that this coupon doesn't carry an expiration date? Therefore, I expect it should be valid indefinitely. Is that not so? I know you value customer service here; so I was wondering if you might be so kind as to honor this offer?"

Clerk (not so confidently): "Well, ah, like I said, that sale ended last week."

Kristin (not as sweetly): "Okay, I understand, but may I please speak to your manager?"

Five minutes later Kristin walks out (a tad triumphantly) with all three T-shirts for fifteen dollars. Meanwhile Janelle is chafing over the delay. All she can think about is that we could have been back in the room an hour ago, eating Reese's Pieces and laughing at Barney Fife on *The Andy Griffith Show* reruns.

It's not that Janelle doesn't like shopping. She just imports her dual life themes of "food and fun" into the shopping experience and then finishes as quickly as possible so she can return to *pure* "food and fun." Recipients of her gifts can count on hers being the most unique under their tree. This year the classic child's game Operation (remember, *bzzzzz*?) was the gift of choice—and not just for the kids. Even her pastor was blessed with this slightly annoying game.

Three girls. Three *very different* girls. And one mom, trying to manage all these competing agendas and maybe even making a memory in the process. Of course, she has a longer list of gifts to buy than all three of us girls put together. But we're kind of high maintenance (can you tell?). By the time she's helped us, she's happy to come home with even one gift or two. That's fine because "making a memory" is her highest priority. It's why she uses the Christmas gift money from Grandma for a hotel room and special meals out. It's why she tries to stimulate meaningful conversation at meals and on shopping breaks.

This can be tricky, as she has had to referee minor rivalries and the tears that we would turn on at a moment's notice (c'mon, we're girls!). But the conflicts and tears usually ended in side-splitting laughter or unforgettable discussions. Although we haven't always made the memories Mom intended, we wouldn't trade those conversations for anything.

In a way the Shopping Trip is like a twenty-four-hour slice of us: mother and daughters. It tells a lot about who we are, how we communicate, and even what we're living for.

What does twenty-four hours in your relationship look like? Mostly tension or mostly fun? More tears or more laughter? More talk of God or more empty words? Are you close friends, or are you worlds apart? Maybe there is nothing but silence.

For every mother and daughter, there is a different and unique relationship. We each have our own distinct strengths and weaknesses, styles, interests, thoughts, and our often-amusing similarities. Being a mom and three daughters, we know this all too well.

If you're a mom with even one girl, you've probably pulled more than a few hairs out trying to understand this "raising daughters" thing. You lie awake at night with mothering questions driving your sleep away: *How do I guide this girl into womanhood? How do I protect her from ungodly influences? How can I keep her from rebelling? How can I help her be passionate for the Lord? How can I remain her friend? How can I get her to really talk?* You may even sometimes wonder why God gave you this particular daughter and what role you are supposed to play in her life. In the end there seem to be more questions than answers, more problems than solutions.

Daughter, you may be skimming this book because your mom is making you read it (caught ya!). Maybe you don't think it's that important to have a relationship with her. Your friends are a lot more fun and easier to talk to. Or maybe you and your mom argue a lot. You wish she understood you better. But you may have a good relationship with your mom—and you want it to be better, like she does. Congratulations. You're mature beyond your years.

But no matter the difficulties in your mother-daughter relationship, the problem isn't the other person. The obstacle isn't a mom who is hard to get along with or a daughter who won't listen. And you can't get to the root of your problems by digging up back issues of parent or teen magazines or tuning into the afternoon talk shows. *A primary source of our trouble is that we have forgotten God's purpose for the mother-daughter relationship.*

This is why as mothers we often have no clear parenting goals. It's why as daughters we sometimes lack appreciation for our mom's involvement in our lives. It's why our relationship sometimes feels like a minefield of touchy subjects, and we run at the first hint of conflict. It's why we lack reasons to talk and something to talk about.

The diagnosis of our problem is found in God's Word, the Bible. After all, He's the one who created the mother-daughter relationship. God's Word speaks to all of us—mothers and daughters. It unravels the tangled issues in our relationships, spans any distance between us, and points the way to rich and meaningful interaction. But more than just helping us get along, the Bible unfolds an exciting and important plan for mothers and daughters: *to pass on the legacy of biblical womanhood that commends the gospel.*

It's within this momentous mission that our questions come to rest, our strife comes to resolution, our loneliness and alienation become companionship and laughter, and our ineffectiveness is revived into usefulness for the gospel.

As we seek to follow God's plan, the pleasant fragrance of Christ will permeate our mother-daughter relationships, extending to the atmosphere of our homes, our churches, and our communities. The aroma will linger long after we are gone. And the enduring effect—in our lifetime and for future generations—will be incalculable (2 Cor. 2:15).

This is our reason to talk. *This* is what we talk about.

The four of us know this is true because we've experienced it. And we've observed its effect in the lives of many mothers and daughters. We're not mother-daughter experts. And we don't think we're anything special—we've had our times of trouble. In fact, we're extraordinarily ordinary. But through the life, death, and resurrection of Jesus Christ, we now have a relationship with God, the Father. Through Him and because of Him we have wonderful, enjoyable relationships with each other.

So please join us for an exciting mother-daughter conversation. We'll share a lot from our own lives (although you might get to know us better than you wanted to!), but most important, we'll look at the Bible and discover the unique purpose that God has for us as mothers and daughters. Carolyn and Nicole have done the writing, but this book is from Kristin's and Janelle's hearts too.

At various points throughout the book we'll shine the spotlight on a mother's responsibility, and at other times we'll focus on a daughter's response. *But all the chapters are for both mothers and daughters.* You may want to sit down and read them together, or you may prefer to take turns reading on your own. If someone is in the habit of marking up her books, you might each want to get your own copy!

No matter how you choose to read this book, "listening in" when the other is addressed will help strengthen your mother-daughter communication. Once you've read a chapter or two, get together and talk about what you've learned. We've provided discussion questions based on the chapters for you, Mom, to use with your daughter (Appendix A).

Sounds easy enough, right? Well, we have to be honest: It won't always be easy. You will probably hit a few bumps in the road. It may be awkward or uncomfortable at times. You may even sin against each other. But don't give up. There is an all-important reason to hang in there and keep talking: A strong, enjoyable, and fruitful relationship awaits you. It will be worth it!

There are 364 days until our next Shopping Trip, but we are hanging out again this morning. We've got a lot more to talk about. In between the chatter and the chores, we are fulfilling God's plan for our relationship. And you can too.

So are you ready for some *girl talk*? Let's get started.

Carolyn *Nicole* *Christi* *Janelle*

PART ONE

The Forging of the Mother-Daughter Bond

1

The Language of Biblical Womanhood

by Carolyn

For hundreds of years, young women who came of age in southern China learned a secret language. Secret, that is, from the men and the boys. Like their mothers and grandmothers before them, these girls were denied the opportunity of learning to read and write Chinese. So the oppressed women of that culture—determined to have a means of expressing themselves—developed their own language. It was a girls-only writing script called Nushu.

According to an article in the *Washington Post*, three days after her wedding a new bride would receive a "Third Day Book," lovingly inscribed in Nushu by her mother, grandmother, and "sworn sisters." In delicate, elongated handwriting these women expressed feelings of sadness at losing a daughter and friend and shared best wishes for her future happiness. The bride would make her own entries in Nushu, and the book became a diary of her married life.

Someday the bride would teach her own daughter Nushu. And so these peasant women preserved their language for over fifteen hundred years, right into our century. With no education, means, or encouragement, they created something unique in all of history: the only language written *by* women *for* women.[1]

Did you know that God has given us our own mother-daughter language? Unlike Nushu, our language is not a secret. It is not a response to oppression, but it is a uniquely feminine language. As mothers and daughters, God has entrusted us with its progress and preservation. It's the language of biblical womanhood.

Biblical womanhood, simply defined, is God's perfect design for women as revealed in the Bible. Much more than a writing script, it's a way of life. More than something we read or write, it's something we speak and do.

We find this language scattered throughout the entire Bible. Tucked in Titus 2:3-5 is a summary of some of the qualities of a godly woman, such as purity, self-control, kindness, love for husband and children, skill in homemaking, and a heart of submission. But we find more traits in passages such as Proverbs 31:10-31, 1 Timothy 5:9-10, and 1 Peter 3:1-6—steadfast faith, good works, strength, and wisdom, united with a gentle and quiet spirit.

Together these characteristics comprise the language of biblical womanhood. They provide for us a composite sketch—to imitate and copy like an aspiring artist would copy a great masterpiece. Throughout this book we'll attempt to trace these lines, to discover what biblical womanhood looks like for a mother and daughter in the twenty-first century.

But first we must understand our responsibility to pass on this language from mother to daughter. For while God clearly calls *all* older women to school the younger women in the art of biblical womanhood (Titus 2:3-5), one of the most important teacher-student relationships is between a mother and her daughter. We have an exciting task, an assignment from God Himself to transfer these feminine attributes from one generation to the next. This is our mother-daughter purpose. Our mission.

I was reminded of our mission earlier this year when my mother sold her house. Because of my father's failing health, my parents recently moved from Florida to Maryland to live with my sister and her family. At my mom's request, my brothers, sisters, and I sorted through all their belongings. She told us to keep or discard whatever we pleased.

I brought several items home for my daughters: some old books for Nicole, a crystal bowl for Kristin, and my grandma's handmade quilt for Janelle. For myself I kept a solitary piece of china, one of the few remaining plates from the set my grandfather bought my mother for her wedding.

I can still remember the set in better days—serving many a guest on a Sunday afternoon. But its comrades have all been broken or have disappeared, and this plate is all I have. It is delicate and faded—you can no longer read the pattern name printed on the back. But it hangs in my dining room as a pleasant reminder of my aging mother's once vivacious hospitality.

My brothers and sisters each took home small items of sentimental value, but don't expect to see us on *Antiques Roadshow* anytime soon. My parents were frugal, modest people who gave away more than they collected. In keeping with her Mennonite background, my mother owned no jewelry except a watch. She never even wore a wedding ring.

Although I have not received costly earthly treasures from my mom, she has given me a gift of priceless value, for she was faithful to pass on to me a legacy of biblical womanhood. Through her teaching and her example she taught me to aspire to these qualities that commend the gospel.

I don't expect to have much of significant monetary value to leave my daughters either. (Maybe one of them can have Mom's china plate if it survives.) But like my mother before me, I want to faithfully impress the qualities of biblical womanhood upon the hearts of my daughters. I want to be found worthy of God's calling to me as their mother, and I want them to live for His glory.

But in order for any of us to do this effectively, our mother-daughter relationships must be strong. This transfer can't be made through a wall of bitterness, amidst yelling and screaming, nor in silence—now can it? In order to pass on the language of biblical womanhood, our relationships must be founded on the Word of God. That's why in the first half of this book we'll consider what the Bible has to say about the mother-daughter relationship, and in the second half we'll discover how a young woman learns to speak the language of biblical womanhood.

The wonderful results of building our relationships on the foundation of God's Word are the joy, peace, fellowship, and fun that make the mother-daughter bond strong. Far from being a duty or an obligation, the mother-daughter relationship can be one of the greatest blessings of our lives.

And it's a strong relationship that will enable us to preserve our unique language. For as you may have noticed, biblical womanhood isn't exactly popular these days. The language our culture speaks is hardly one of selflessness, purity, submission, or faith. Instead, it demeans these attributes and the gospel they commend. Our culture speaks a "live for the moment, live for yourself" language that misses out on the beauty of biblical womanhood.

What is truly troublesome, however, is that many Christian mothers and daughters have dismissed the language of biblical womanhood or are wholly unfamiliar with it. They speak the language of the world—often unintentionally—by believing that submission is outdated, purity is impossible, and homemaking is unappealing.

Maybe *you* too think these ideas are a little old-fashioned. You're not sure you want to speak the language of biblical womanhood. But allow us to introduce you to these feminine traits again. You may be surprised at how much they relate to what you're going through and what a difference they will make in your life.

Our language points to and highlights the most joyous news in all of history: the gospel of Jesus Christ. Paul says in Titus 2:10 that these qualities "adorn the doctrine of God our Savior." They declare to the world that the Bible is true, that Jesus is real, and that the gospel is the power of God to change lives. Biblical womanhood displays the truth that "God so loved the world, that he gave his only Son, that whoever believes in him should not perish but have eternal life" (John 3:16).

This task isn't reserved for an elite group of extraordinary mothers and daughters. It's been assigned to forgiven sinners like you and me. None of us on our own is capable of displaying even one small aspect of biblical womanhood—much less passing it on into the future. But through the power of the gospel we can speak this language and "shine as lights in the world" (Phil. 2:15).

This must be the aspiration of all mothers and daughters: the successful transfer of the qualities of biblical womanhood that sparkle with the gospel—so that in the midst of this me-centered, self-focused, ungodly language of our culture, we can speak the refreshingly pure, altogether true, and saving message of Jesus Christ.

Imperfect Makes Perfect

by Nicole

D on't try to talk to my mom while she is on the telephone. She firmly believes in doing one thing at a time and doing it well. I, on the other hand, have mastered the art of doing three things at once—all poorly. Mom, she drinks her coffee black. Me, I add more sugar than is put in your average cotton candy. My mom is graceful, poised, and calm. I'm expressive, sporadic, clumsy, and (according to my sisters) a little crazy. When Mom talks, everyone listens. I talk so much that people often tune me out like elevator music. Mom's favorite meal is roast beef, green beans, mashed potatoes with gravy, and strawberry shortcake. She's a southern gal. But give me a plate of sushi with extra wasabi and a cup of hot green tea. I'm a suburban girl.

I'm sure we're related; people sometimes say we look alike. I know I will never be as pretty as she is, but I tell them, "If only I could be godly like her, then I'd be happy."

With all our differences, I didn't always understand my mom. I suspect she didn't always know what to make of me either. Really, it's a miracle we're such good friends today.

Maybe you can relate. Maybe you and your mother are as different as, well, roast beef and sushi. Maybe you have no common interests or style of communication; so you just don't talk much.

Or maybe your differences go deeper than silly preferences. So when you do try to talk, conflict inevitably flares up. You've allowed real disagreements to wedge between you, and they are slowly but steadily pushing you apart. Perhaps a little question occasionally rings the doorbell of your mind: "How did you end up being related to *her*?" The answer: God set it up that way.

He has created *your* mother-daughter relationship. He doesn't just put mothers and daughters together like a guy in a deli slapping meat and cheese on bread. God has placed us in the exact mother-daughter relationship that He desires. Psalm 139 informs us of this: "In your book were written, every one of them, the days that were formed for me, when as yet there were none of them" (v. 16).

Now we don't usually apply this verse to the family God has arranged for us. But think about it—if *all* your days were ordained, including the day you were born, then whom you were born to (or, moms, who was born to you) is no accident.

This fact is confirmed in Acts 17:26 (NIV): "From one man he made every nation of men . . . and he determined the times set for them and *the exact places where they should live."*

God doesn't make mistakes. As my sister Janelle likes to quip, "There wasn't a mix-up in the children's department in heaven. An angel did not inform the Lord, 'Ah, Lord, we messed up, and Nicole, she was supposed to be a part of the Smith family, but she accidentally got put in the Mahaney family.'" Not so!

The exact family we were placed in—the exact mother and the exact daughter we have received—were prearranged by God before the first day of creation. And if you are adopted or have a stepmother, God was equally sovereign in His choice for you. He specially selected the woman who is now your mother with precise detail and matchless love.

And God in His love granted us unique abilities, gifts, talents, and strengths that benefit each other. Moms, your daughters are a heritage, a reward from God (Ps. 127:3). They are not a bother, a burden, or a problem—but a reward! Your daughter (and not so and so's daughter) is the perfect girl for you. And, daughter, this works two ways: Your mother is also the perfect mom for you. I don't mean that she is perfect. None of us is. Only God is perfect. But because He doesn't make mistakes, I can confidently assert that your mom's the right mom for you. Whether you realize it or not, God has given you a good gift.

I must pause here, for some of you may have trouble swallowing the truth that God's goodness was at work in arranging *your* mother-daughter relationship. Perhaps you have a mother who is not a Christian or, worse, whose behavior causes you great heartache and trouble. She may be an alcoholic, verbally berating, or physically abusive (for those of you in this situation, please seek counsel from your pastor and, if necessary, protection by the authorities). Your mom may have abandoned you, leaving you desperately confused, alone, and shouldering heavy responsibilities. The one person you would expect to love you best has hurt you most.

Or maybe you are a mother whose daughter's rebellion has caused deep pain and sorrow. She has turned her back on you and on God; she is angry, rebellious, and unkind. Your attempts to show love have only invited further insults and greater hatred. Her lifestyle is wreaking havoc in your family, and you don't know where it will end. Maybe, in the quiet moments, you wish you'd never had a daughter.

So how could a loving God have chosen *your* mother or daughter? You are at a loss to understand.

While I can't begin to comprehend your suffering, there is a story in the Bible that can help you gain understanding. You may recall the account of Joseph found in the book of Genesis. As a young man he experienced great harm from his family—in fact, his brothers sold him into slavery. But Joseph understood that God's sovereign love was at work for good even through the malicious actions of his brothers.

From slavery, and by way of prison, Joseph eventually

became powerful in the land of Egypt and saved his people from famine. He later told his brothers, "As for you, you meant evil against me, but God meant it for good, to bring it about that many people should be kept alive" (Gen. 50:20).

Whether or not your mother or daughter intends her actions for evil against you, she cannot thwart God's intentions. God has a plan, a *gracious* plan, for your mother-daughter relationship. Just as He used Joseph's sufferings to save a nation, He is more than able to bring forth astonishing good from your trials. So may I urge you to put your trust in our sovereign God? Even now His purposes are at work in your mother-daughter relationship.

For all of us, the guarantee that God has ordained our mother-daughter relationship for good provides the hope we need to resolve any conflict and surmount any challenge. There is no problem in our relationship that causes God to rethink whether or not He got it right by putting us together. So neither should we question it.

God actually uses each other's limitations, flaws, and peculiarities to help us grow in godliness. The habits that annoy or embarrass us, the sins that tempt us to anger or resentment, and the views and opinions we don't understand about one another—all these were custom designed to help us grow in biblical womanhood. I love what Mr. Knightly says in the matchmaking comedy *Emma*: "Maybe it is our imperfections which make us so perfect for one another!"[1]

My mom and I have experienced this dynamic in our relationship. One thing you need to know about Mom is that she loves peace, order, and structure. She would say that she tends to love it too much. By contrast, I didn't always appreciate my mom's love for order. Thus my disorderly, haphazard way of living was a source of tension at times when I lived at home.

But things have changed since I have gotten married. Now that I have a family of my own, I love an orderly schedule and a clean house—almost as much as Mom. I'm always calling her for useful tips to simplify my life. I appreciate this strength of her character like never before. But she would also say that God used her daughters (and primarily me) to help her overcome an excessive concern with a clean and organized house. We've both grown in godly character, thanks to our God-ordained differences.

God didn't design the mother-daughter relationship *primarily* so we could feel comfortable, like each other, and get along. As we learned in the previous chapter, He has a much higher purpose in mind. He intends for us to display and pass along biblical womanhood so that we can bring honor to the gospel.

If you grasp this truth—that God has handpicked your mother or your daughter—it can revolutionize your relationship. It settles any doubts about its validity, provides hope amidst mother-daughter conflict, and gives confidence to accomplish God's grand purpose together, by His grace.

So the next time that pesky little question, "Why her?" casts doubt on the origin of your mother-daughter relationship, slam the door in its face. *God* has ordained this relationship. You are the perfect combination for passing on the language of biblical womanhood.

Cover Mom

I picked up the latest copy of a popular teen magazine the other day. I was looking for someone, but I couldn't find her.

Here's what I did find: "419 ways to be beautiful" (what kind of random number is that?), foolproof ways to "get great hair," and my "love horoscope." The cover was plastered with a close-up of—surprise, surprise—a beautiful actress. What more could a girl want than advice on love, hair, beauty, and some gossip about a celebrity? At least that's what the editors seem to assume is the base level of a teenage girl's interests.

I was looking for Mom, but I couldn't find her. She didn't even make the back page. From boyfriends to prom dresses, from acne to hairstyles, Mom was nowhere to be found. There were plenty of friends and plenty of boys and plenty of advice from "experts." They even had a kind of "phone-a-mom" replacement named Julie (not her real name), but no Mom.

It made me mad. I wanted to have my own little magazine-burning right there in the bookstore. I wanted to write a letter to the editor. But that wouldn't do any good. Besides, it's not only magazines. Television, movies, and other media for teens frequently portray a motherless society. The world they depict is largely peer-centered with a few mom-replacements on the side.

If you had only teen magazines and television as guides, it would appear that moms are a thing of the past—gone the way of eight-tracks and record players. Apparently, girls no longer have mothers to steer them through the often confusing and tumultuous teenage years.

But actually girls have simply been duped by the cultural lie that Mom doesn't understand and can't relate. Of course, she's good for making dinner, buying school supplies, and driving them to and from friends' houses and swim meets. But go to her for advice? Look to her for support? This hasn't occurred to them.

Modern teenage girls often avoid or even resist their moms' involvement in their lives. They view mothers as basically irrelevant when it comes to their concerns, decisions, and aspirations. Consequently, when was the last time you went into a teenage girl's room and saw a life-size poster of her mom on the wall? Sad to say, many young women miss out on one of God's main channels of wisdom, comfort, and blessing just when they need it most.

Adding to the problem, many moms have faded into the background without complaint. They think being an "understanding" mom entails giving their daughters space, encouraging their peer relationships, and not prying too much into their personal lives. They just try to love their daughters in hopes that they'll open up someday. These moms are hesitant to exercise their authority or get involved in their daughters' lives.

This approach is not limited to our ungodly culture. It's increasingly common in the church as well. One sincere and godly woman who has a wonderful ministry to girls nevertheless resigns herself to this faulty view when she writes, "The influence of positive peer relations in a group of girls cannot be overemphasized. A parent's influence during adolescence is limited. Not all girls will allow their parents to make a difference in their lives at this time. Friends will have the greatest impact."[1]

However, if we as mothers and daughters want to speak the language of biblical womanhood, we must start by bringing Mom's role into focus. Although mom-as-bystander is a common notion, I want to introduce you to an alternative viewpoint: God's view of parents as presented in the Bible.

In His Word, God opens up a whole, new exciting world of parent-child relating. Verse after verse insists that Mom and Dad play an active and primary role in their children's lives. Take Proverbs as an example. It fairly explodes with instructions to the son [and daughter] to "Hear . . . your father's instruction, and forsake not your mother's teaching" and to "receive [your parents'] words and treasure . . . [their] commandments" (Prov. 1:8; 2:1; 3:1; 4:1, 10, 20, etc.).

Author Paul Tripp comments, "God essentially says this: 'I have designed *the family* to be my primary learning community. There is no better context to teach the truths that need to be taught so that my people would live the way they should live'"[2] (emphasis added).

So classrooms, youth groups, and friends—though beneficial—are not the *primary* learning community. It is the family. It's Dad, and it's Mom. Why? Dr. Tripp goes on to explain: "Parents have unique opportunities to instruct their children, opportunities no one else will have, because parents live with them."[3] God has set children up with the best possible help right in their own homes. And while Dad's leadership role is essential in the family, we want to look at Mom's role in this chapter—after all, this is a mother-daughter book. (But we didn't forget about fathers. My dad, C. J. Mahaney, has written "A Word to Fathers" at the conclusion of this book.)

God has chosen Mom to be our primary teacher, to be the foremost influence in our young lives. She possesses wisdom from God for us, and He has chosen her to impart the language of biblical womanhood. (Keep in mind that in the second half of this book we'll examine the topics that comprise our language. You will have the opportunity to learn these qualities from your mom.)

When we pay close attention to our moms' teaching, the Bible predicts a splendid outcome: ". . . for length of days and

years of life and peace they will add to you. . . . you will find favor
and good success in the sight of God and man" (Prov. 3:2, 4).
Following our mothers' teaching will launch us into a lifetime
of blessing and honor. What a sweet deal!

If you are reading carefully, you may notice who is *not* men-
tioned in any of these verses: substitute moms and peer relationships. Indeed, Proverbs often warns of the dangers of
ungodly peer influence: "The companion of fools will suffer
harm" (Prov. 13:20).

Now I am not advocating that you abandon all peer or
other adult friendships. *Godly* relationships are gifts from our
heavenly Father. A prudent mom will seek to position her
daughter to benefit from the encouragement and example of
other believers.

I also recognize that some young women may lack the spiritual guidance of a Christian mother. Maybe you've lost your
mother, or maybe your mom is not a Christian or is an immature believer whom you can't rely on for godly advice. You may
find yourself discouraged as you read this book; you wonder
how you'll ever learn to speak the language of biblical womanhood without a mother to teach you. But do not despair—you
have not been left out.

In Titus 2:3-5 God directs all older women to train the
younger women in the qualities of biblical womanhood. And
God never issues a command that is not accompanied by the
support we need to see it through. You are not hindered from
learning our feminine language because you do not have a godly
mom. God will supply another woman to teach you. He knows
every detail of your situation, and nothing will impede His purposes in your life.

So pray right now, and ask Him to provide a mentor. You are
simply praying God's Word back to Him. You are asking for His
assistance to obey His Word. Imagine how eager He is to answer
this request.

Then go in search of a godly woman to train you in biblical

womanhood. This may be your pastor's wife, or she could possibly recommend someone else. But have confidence—God will surely provide.

However, when God does provide a young woman with a godly mother, the daughter must not neglect her mother's teaching. A wise mother's influence, guidance, and instruction are special blessings from God that we should enthusiastically embrace.

So, daughters, where is Mom in the magazine of your life? Is she on hand for all the important issues? Is she nearby in the pages of struggle and confusion? Does she pop up amidst your questions and decisions? Does Mom grace the front cover of your magazine?

Maybe you're not sure if your mom is the primary influence in your life. How about taking the following quiz to find out?

- ❀ Who is the first person you go to with a problem or a question?
- ❀ Whose opinion matters most to you?
- ❀ Whose counsel and advice do you respect the most?
- ❀ Whom do you go to for comfort in difficult times?
- ❀ Whom do you look to for guidance and direction?
- ❀ Who is the most influential teacher in your life?

If Mom was not the answer to most or all of these questions, then whoever *was* is probably the primary influence in your life—whether you've realized it or not. And, chances are, you're missing out on the benefits that follow from your mom's teaching.

So please don't wait another moment. Bring Mom into the content of your life. This may be a new idea for you, but start by doing something simple. Begin by talking to your mom. Share with her what you've been thinking about lately, and tell her that you desire for her to be your primary mentor. I am confident that God will bless even this small step.

Moms, maybe you find the responsibility to be your daughter's primary teacher quite daunting. If so, remember that *God* has called you to be her mother. And when God calls, He enables. God created the position of motherhood and hired you as His employee. Unlike a human boss, He doesn't merely provide you some training, throw you a manual, and expect you to perform this task on your own. Rather, He supplies all the wisdom, strength, insight, encouragement, hope, creativity, help, and grace you could possibly need to teach the language of biblical womanhood to your daughter.

So don't hang back and wait for your daughter to come to you. With confidence in God's abundant grace, step up and begin to impart wisdom and instruction to her.

And finally, girls, don't forget the book of Proverbs' predictions. If we heed our mother's advice and receive her teaching, we will find peace, favor, and good success (Prov. 3:2, 4). So let's ask for God's help to put Mom back on the front cover where she belongs.

Afternoon Out

by Carolyn

It was Afternoon Out, our weekly time as mother and daughters. The problem was, only two of us wanted to be there. The other two, Nicole and Kristin, sat at opposite ends of the backseat staring out their respective windows, slouched shoulders and blank expressions saying what words did not. Janelle and I chatted in the front seat for a while, but their non-participation was impossible to ignore.

I suppressed the impulse to turn the car around and expel them both to walk the rest of the way home. Instead, I breathed a prayer for the Holy Spirit's help and broke the silence.

"Okay, girls," I began, "what's going on?"

"Nothing," came the predictably weak reply.

I wasn't about to let it go at that. After several more probing questions, they finally admitted they would rather be doing something else. Basically, they lacked any enthusiasm for being with their mom.

I wasn't prepared for my daughters' attitude change toward me when they reached the teen years. What happened to the little girls who would jump up and down with glee just to go to McDonalds with their mom? And it seemed only a short time ago that they were excited about my husband's idea for Afternoon Out. He would watch Chad, our infant son, so I could take the girls out for lunch and an activity. Somewhere along the way, however, their excitement had waned.

Conventional wisdom would tell me that this is normal teenage behavior and that a smart mom should back off when her daughter reaches this stage. She must accept that her daughter needs to express her independence, spread her wings, and become who she was meant to be. She must give her space and not take it personally. If her daughter doesn't feel like talking to her, that's okay—so say many of the "experts."

But informed by Scripture, Paul Tripp suggests that this strategy is a mistake:

> Sadly, I am afraid, many parents accept the moat that teenagers tend to build around themselves. They adjust to the lack of time and relationship with their teen who, only a few short years ago, wanted to tag along with them everywhere they went. They quit talking when their teenager quits talking. So, at the point where significant things happen, which the teenager was never meant to deal with alone, Mom and Dad are nowhere to be found.[1]

I'll admit it. At first I was sorely tempted to "accept the moat" separating me from my daughters. It was not much fun forcing them to spend time with me or talk to me when they didn't want to. It was the last thing I wanted to do. Oh, how I wished I could take Janelle out and leave the other two at home until they begged to come back!

What kept me from doing that was God's command for me to be the primary influence in their lives. As we read in the last chapter, we are to teach and instruct our daughters in the ways of the Lord (Prov. 1:8). This includes the successful hand-off of the language of biblical womanhood.

We can't toss these qualities to our daughters from a distance. We can't declare "mission accomplished" after a few one-hour training sessions as if we were teaching a basic computer program. Biblical womanhood is transferred through our example, our speech, and by teaching these virtues in the nitty-gritty of everyday life.

This process requires a *relationship*. Clearly, for me to exert any meaningful influence in my daughters' lives, I must be close to them. I must be *consistently*, *actively*, and *intimately* involved in their world. And while this is important at any stage, it is absolutely crucial during the teenage years. As a mom, I had to press in all the more intently during this pivotal season, whether my daughters eagerly received my friendship and guidance or stubbornly resisted it.

Daughters, may I urge you not to resist your mom's involvement in your life? If you have built a moat around your heart, you have not cut off an enemy but a friend. A friend, I might add, who has the essential tools you need to navigate the teen years. She isn't perfect, I know, but I am almost certain she is lovingly committed to being your friend so that she can lead you in the ways of the Lord. That is probably why she has you reading this book together. So don't stop talking, but open your heart to her friendship: It is your ticket to wisdom, counsel, and a whole storehouse of God's blessings.

Moms, our daughters were not meant to deal with the myriad of teenage trials alone. Contrary to popular opinion, this is precisely when they need us most. Not only do they acutely require our advice, correction, and leadership, but they also need our friendship, encouragement, and comforting presence on the road to godliness. Our daughters don't arrive at Destination Maturity on their thirteenth birthday. Rather, they are being propelled into a period of serious growth potential. The vital significance of a mother's godly influence and friendship during these years cannot be overstated.

I can imagine you responding out loud to me as you read this chapter. "Okay, Carolyn," you say, "I'm convinced that I need to be involved in my daughter's life. I want to be a faithful mom, but she won't let me get close to her. What am I to do?"

While I don't pretend to hold the key to a young girl's heart, I know the one who does. As mothers we must appeal directly to the throne of almighty God. Proverbs 21:1 discloses: "The king's heart is a stream of water in the hand of the LORD; he turns it wherever he will." The sovereign God who directs the hearts of kings and presidents holds *our* daughters' hearts in His hand.

If your daughter has constructed a moat around her heart—or if you fear she might—you must first make your request to the Heart-Keeper. No moat or barrier is too difficult for Him to overcome. Prayer is a key to access your daughter's heart.

Author J. C. Ryle encouraged parents: "The Lord is far more willing to hear than we to pray; far more ready to give blessings than we to ask them;—but He loves to be entreated for them. . . . I suspect the child of many prayers is seldom cast away."[2] The truth is, God is more than able and more than inclined to soften our daughters' hearts. So let us, with faith and boldness, ask Him to restore or strengthen our mother-daughter relationships.

We must seek the Lord, and we must take action. We must put our boots on and wade into the details of our daughters' lives. It is not wise to allow them to set the agenda for our relationships. Backed by Scripture's mandate, we must press in and pursue their hearts and affection.

Now this doesn't mean we come with our fingers wagging and tell our daughters—*you will be my friend whether you like it or not!* As I once heard a pastor say, "Friendship is earned, not demanded."

And friendship doesn't mean that we relinquish our God-given authority. Rather, our authority is the foundation on which we are to build our friendship. The goal is to win our daughters' hearts and affection so we can lead them in the ways of the Lord.

To earn their friendship, we must first earn their trust. We must approach our daughters with humility and ask questions. We can't assume that we know the reasons they may keep us at arm's length. Judging them will only push them further away.

Maybe we have unwittingly offended them, or they are bitter over a decision we have made. Or perhaps their reaction is simply the consequence of a worldly view of mothers. In many cases their hearts may have grown proud. They may also fear what their friends would think about their hanging out with Mom. Or they might be unaware that their attitude and behavior have changed.

When I queried my daughters about their reasons for pushing me away, many of these answers came tumbling out. So we had some long and important conversations about my God-assigned role in their lives. We discussed why rejecting my influence was displeasing to God and would be to their detriment. I told them again and again how much I loved them and that I was eager to be their friend.

We had these conversations repeatedly over a period of time, until by God's grace my daughters' hearts began to turn toward me. Communication—constant talking—was indispensable in building a friendship with them. (We'll look at five characteristics of effective communication in the next chapter.)

Nicole and Kristin also admitted that they disliked Afternoon Out because it frequently included correction of some kind. They were right. What I had intended to be a time for making fun mother-daughter memories had become a discipline session. So I needed to make a change. I purposed to save the serious discussions for later and keep Afternoon Out primarily devoted to fun. Humbly admitting that I was wrong was an entryway into my daughters' hearts.

Let me address a specific group of women for a moment—those who fear that the doors of their daughters' hearts may have closed forever. Maybe they are grown and gone, or are still at home and yet seemingly their hearts are out of reach. The guilt and regret you feel has been mounting with every page you turn. *If only I had heard these truths when my daughters were younger,* you lament. *Maybe things would have turned out differently.* But now you fear it is too late.

This couldn't be further from the truth. There is always hope for your relationship to be restored. We serve a faithful God whose steadfast love never ceases and whose mercies never come to an end. They are new every morning (Lam. 3:22-23).

Our Lord's faithfulness should give you renewed courage and resolve to approach your daughter again.

Go in humility. Invite her to share her grievances. Ask for her forgiveness. Demonstrate God's love to her in spite of her resistance. Although this may not be easy, you can trust that God will reward your efforts as a mother. He will receive glory from your faith and obedience to Him, and you will be a shining example of biblical womanhood to your daughter.

Finally, in order to bridge the moat that our daughters may have built (or to keep them from building one), we must make the mother-daughter relationship one of our highest priorities. After our relationship with God and our husbands, nothing should receive more attention, focus, and time.

Moms, please be wise with your expectations. I can tell you now that developing a friendship with your daughter will take some time. When my daughters became teenagers, the changes in them caught me (and other moms I know) by surprise. It seemed that overnight life got more complicated. One day they were playing outside with the neighborhood kids where the biggest problem was a dispute over whose turn it was to be "it." The next day their bodies were changing, they had a crush on a boy, and their emotions were all over the map.

I quickly realized that the serene days of childhood were over. This was a whole new ballgame. I began to see that I needed to devote significantly more time to my daughters. So I spent less time with friends, service projects in the church, and leisure activities. I pared down my schedule to create opportunities to talk and be available when my girls wanted to talk.

Even secular moms are realizing that teenagers need more of their time. I recently read a newspaper article that profiled career women who were coming home, not to care for their toddlers but for their teenagers. Susan Dykstra, an "investment analyst, vice president," and "high-energy career woman" returned to work as a young mom soon after giving birth to her babies. But then her babies became teenage boys. "At the very stage when parents often expect to be providing less attention, Dykstra and her husband thought their family needed more." So she "packed up the files, stepped off the corporate track [and] . . . became a stay-at-home mom."[3]

A researcher from the Harvard School of Public Health is quoted in the article: "We've tended to think that it's okay for parents to step back a little and let other adults play more of a role. The research doesn't support that."[4] The article goes on to conclude: "Savvy parents realize *teenagers require as much attention as toddlers*"[5] (emphasis added).

As Christian mothers, of course our aspirations are higher than simply being "savvy moms." We want to glorify God and pass on the language of biblical womanhood to our daughters. And I am not advocating that we look to the local newspaper for guidance in parenting. Scripture is our ultimate and authoritative guide. But I do believe these parents have come to a realization—in a limited way—of this truth affirmed in Scripture: As our daughters mature, they require *more and not less* attention, training, instruction, correction, and encouragement.

Now for single moms, I know that intentional mothering requires exceptional sacrifice on your part. But God will give you ample strength as you look to Him (Ps. 28:7; 2 Cor. 12:9). And although you may not be able to stay home with your daughters, He will graciously multiply your efforts to teach them the language of biblical womanhood.

During my daughters' teenage years, I often felt as tired as when my children were small and I existed on coffee and cat naps. It was a sacrifice of sleep, leisure time, and much energy, but it was worth it.

Suffice it to say, I wouldn't trade the relationship I have with my daughters today for all the nights of sleep in the world. After my husband, they are my three closest friends. And as a testimony to God's grace, Nicole and Kristin now thank me for pressing in even though they had tried to push me away. Today although they are married, we still continue the Afternoon Out tradition once a month. In fact, Nicole and Kristin are unhappy with me when we *don't* have Afternoon Out.

For Further Study

❀ *Age of Opportunity: A Biblical Guide to Parenting Teens* by Paul David Tripp

❀ *The Duties of Parents* by J. C. Ryle

❀ *Shepherding a Child's Heart* by Tedd Tripp

❀ "Parents, Teens, and Reasonable Expectations" audio series by Grant Layman, available at www.sovereigngraceministries.org

5

Constant Communication

by Carolyn

Talking is what teenage girls do best. They're professionals. They talk to friends on the phone, strangers who will listen, the dog, or even to themselves. When it comes to talking to Mom, however, conversation may not come so readily. Does this sample conversation sound familiar?

"How was school today, honey?"

"Fine."

"What did you learn?"

"Not much."

"Who did you talk to?"

"No one really."

"Is anything wrong?"

"No."

Gripping dialogue, isn't it? Actually it falls far short of God's intention for mother-daughter communication. We read of His remarkable pattern for our talking in the book of Deuteronomy, immediately after the Israelites received the Ten Commandments. There God commanded with majesty and authority:

Hear, O Israel: the LORD our God, the LORD is one. You shall love the LORD your God with all your heart and with all your soul and with all your might. And these words that I command you today shall be on your heart. You shall teach them diligently to your children, and shall talk of them when you sit in your house, and when you walk by the way, and when you lie down, and when you rise. *You shall bind them as a sign on your hand, and they shall be as frontlets between your eyes. You shall write them on the doorposts of your house and on your gates. (Deut. 6:4-9, emphasis added)*

From examining these verses and dipping into one or two others, I want to suggest five principles for *girl talk*: mother-daughter communication that speaks the language of biblical womanhood. Along the way I will recount my own journey of communication with my daughters.

My girls, I have to say, can keep pace with the best of talkers. Janelle even spends half the night talking in her sleep (*those are some interesting conversations!*). However, as you discovered in the last chapter, we also had our share of communication crashes.

I certainly don't consider myself an exceptional mom. I tried a lot of things that didn't work. However, I hope these truths from God's Word and practical suggestions will serve to shape and define your communication with each other.

The first thing to note from these verses is that parents are chiefly responsible to initiate communication with their children: "You shall teach them diligently to your children, and shall talk of them" (Deut. 6:7). Mothers, *we* are accountable to God to promote conversation with our daughters. If there is only token interaction between us, we must assume responsibility to reverse that trend. Godly communication isn't a happy accident. It is only possible by the grace of God, but it requires faithful effort on the part of us moms. So the first *girl talk* principle is: *Godly mother-daughter communication starts with Mom.*

Daughters, you are by no means off the hook. Picture an asterisk next to this principle. While your mom has primary responsibility for communication, you should not simply wait for her to take the initiative. Rather, you should initiate communication as well. If you are going to benefit from your mother's wisdom and counsel, then talking and listening are a must.

At first, in my daughters' early teenage years, I was the one having to initiate most of our significant discussions. Sometimes the dialogue went smoothly; other times it was quite discouraging. But I knew that I wasn't allowed to give up.

Setting aside times for Afternoon Out, dates with each daughter, and yearly overnights helped to ensure that communication remained a priority. I realized that in order to have particular important conversations, I needed to put them on the calendar. Often I prepared specific questions, words of encouragement, or topics to discuss on these occasions. To be sure, there were instances when these plans went awry; however, this practice did generate many profitable hours of communication.

From time to time my daughters brushed aside my efforts to talk or probe their thoughts. Occasionally they felt awkward, and I had to wait patiently till they were ready to divulge. Sometimes they were happy to chat about trivial stuff but hesitant to share what was on their hearts. My daughters quickly learned, however, that "I dunno" wasn't an acceptable answer. Though it wasn't always easy, I sought to lovingly persevere and promote godly conversation.

At some point, and almost without my realizing it, our mother-daughter communication took on a life of its own. The silence and reluctance gave way to an unending stream of conversation that hasn't stopped to this day. In fact, my role now is primarily as listener. I no longer need to ask many questions before the truth comes pouring out.

So, moms, I want to cheer you on in your efforts to improve communication with your daughters. I know it takes much time and great skill to draw out the thoughts of their hearts, but God will not fail to bless your labors. And, girls, may I encourage you to make communication easy for your moms? Why not surprise them by taking the initiative to talk? Constant communication isn't just your moms' desire; it is God's intention for your relationships.

Our mother-daughter relationship is actually to be one long, running conversation interrupted by the likes of school, church, and sleep. *Girl talk* should be squeezed into every available moment of the day: ". . . when you sit in your house, and when you walk by the way, and when you lie down, and when you rise" (Deut. 6:7). This just about covers it, wouldn't you say? In every place and at every time of day we are to be talking to each other. So the second *girl talk* principle is: *Godly mother-daughter communication happens all the time.* This means we shouldn't wait until a crisis or only for the scheduled times. We are to be talking constantly.

Conversation with my daughters often began the moment I awoke and concluded well past my ideal bedtime. Sometimes it started during my morning devotions when a daughter would hesitantly knock and ask to chat. Frequently one or more of the girls would join me as I got ready for the day, borrowing my mascara and gabbing all the while. Talking continued as the girls popped in and out from one activity or another. And dinnertime often lasted well into the evening as we enjoyed many memorable family discussions. By being home and being available, I was able to foster ongoing conversation.

But for single moms and women who don't have the option to be home with your children, remember that God will assist you to make the most of each moment that you *do* have.

Deuteronomy 6 prescribes not only the frequency of our mother-daughter conversation but the content of our talks as well: "These words that I command you today shall be on your heart. You shall teach them diligently to your children, and shall talk of them" (v. 6). We shouldn't try to have good communication simply so we can experience a happy and peaceful relationship. Our conversation should be centered around the most important topic of all, God and His Word. Thus our third and most significant *girl talk* principle is: *Godly mother-daughter communication is about the Word of God.*

And for mothers and daughters, talking about the Word of God includes our language of biblical womanhood. Communication with my daughters touched almost constantly on one aspect of biblical womanhood or another—whether it was the fear of the Lord, purity in their interactions with guys, or how they dressed or cared for their appearance. I didn't say, "We're going to talk about biblical womanhood now;" rather, it was the thread that ran through all our conversations.

These conversations took place before and after social events, church meetings, or any other activity outside the home. I tried to prepare my girls for the temptations they were likely to encounter: for example, trying to attract a certain boy's attention or tolerating gossip. I also coached them to enter any setting poised to serve, to reach out to others, and to set a godly example.

When they arrived at home, we would debrief—if not that night, then first thing the next morning. I sought to be faithful to keep them accountable to their commitments to display biblical womanhood. I praised them for demonstrations of godly character. And my daughters would often disclose temptations they had faced. Together we discussed their conduct, and, if necessary, I would send them back to confront or encourage a friend.

While God's Word is of first importance, this doesn't mean we must only talk about spiritual things. My daughters and I have had plenty of frivolous conversations about current events, hair problems, or whatever crazy predicament Nicole has gotten herself into lately. These don't make up the primary substance of our conversation, and they aren't the primary goal. But the light-hearted chatter forms a relational platform from which to address more serious issues. And today there is really no line between what's serious and what's fun. Both are jumbled together in one delightful mix.

Also vital to the transfer of biblical womanhood is truthful communication. That leads us to the fourth *girl talk* principle: *Godly mother-daughter communication is open and honest*. First John 1:7 insists: "If we walk in the light, as he is in the light, we have fellowship with one another, and the blood of Jesus his Son cleanses us from all sin."

Again, moms, we must work vigorously to set a standard of humility and transparency. As one wise author says of parenting: "It involves investing your life in your child in open and honest communication that unfolds the meaning and purpose of life. It is not simply direction, but direction in which there is self-disclosure and sharing. Values and spiritual vitality are not simply taught, but caught."[1]

To help our daughters catch the beauty of biblical womanhood, we must inject our conversations with personal confession and humility and admit where we fall short of God's perfect design. If we proudly seek to present a faultless image, our daughters may well throw up their hands in despair. But when we share our own sins and also our experiences of God's mercy on the sometimes-bumpy trail to godliness, it will encourage our daughters to persevere. Although we must employ wisdom in determining what is appropriate to disclose, our honest communication will make it easy for them to share their own temptations and sins.

Girls, may I implore you to be truthful and honest with your mom? If you are hiding any sin from her, you are headed for trouble. You may think your mom will never find out. But someone already knows. God knows. David confesses in Psalm 69:5: "O God, you know my folly; the wrongs I have done are not hidden from you." Deceiving your mom is like pretending God can't see. It's living in a make-believe world where sin has no consequences. But the Bible tells us that in the real world, "the wages of sin is death" (Rom. 6:23) and that "your sin will find you out" (Num. 32:23).

However, by confessing your sin to God and to your mom,

you can admit the truth that God sees and thus avoid these dire consequences. This is "walking in the light." As a way to encourage my daughters to be open and honest, I would periodically ask, "Is there anything that you need to tell me?" So let me also ask you, "Is there anything that you need to tell your mom?" When you admit your sin, you will experience fellowship with your mom and with God. And best of all, the Bible says, "If we confess our sins, [God] is faithful and just to forgive us our sins and to cleanse us from all unrighteousness" (1 John 1:9).

Now for all you moms who have been sinking deeper into discouragement with each successive *girl talk* principle, please do not lose heart! While constant communication about the ways of the Lord is certainly hard work, you are not without help. May the fifth and final *girl talk* principle buoy your soul, for: *Godly mother-daughter communication is possible through the grace of God.*

You will probably have days when it seems your communication is regressing instead of progressing (I certainly did!). Or you may be deadlocked in a conflict that prevents you from moving forward in meaningful conversation (we'll discuss this obstacle in the next chapter). But no barrier or challenge is insurmountable with God.

He can take our faltering conversations and flawed efforts and transform them into rich communication that brings glory to Him. He reminds us: "My grace is sufficient for you, for my power is made perfect in weakness" (2 Cor. 12:9). Pastor Charles Spurgeon elaborated: "He gives grace abundantly, seasonably, constantly, readily, sovereignly. . . . He generously pours into [our] souls without ceasing, and He always will do so, whatever may occur."[2]

You see, in God is available the all-sufficient grace we need. Let's admit our inadequacies to Him and ask for His blessing on our mother-daughter communication. So why don't we put this book down and spend some time talking with our daughters.

P.S. In addition to discussion questions for this chapter, we've compiled a list of questions for moms to ask daughters and daughters to ask moms. You'll find these conversation starters in Appendix B.

For Further Study

❀ *War of Words: Getting to the Heart of Your Communication Struggles* by Paul David Tripp

Conflict Jungle

by Nicole

I don't understand what the big deal is! I huffed to myself, only half listening to my mom's lecture as I prepared my defense. *Haven't I heard this speech somewhere before? Oh yeah, it was yesterday. I didn't clean up my room then either. According to Mom, this has been happening a lot lately. I think* pattern *is the word she's looking for. It's a word she uses a lot.*

Mom was not pleased with me. Being the discerning girl I was, I could tell. I'd really tested her patience this time. But I was angry too. I couldn't understand why she was making such a fuss. *Why does she insist that everything has to be done in a peaceful and orderly way, exactly as she likes it? Why does she have to make these silly rules? After all, I have a busy life. And I'm not an orderly kind of person. All I want is for her to understand and give me a little space. Can't she let me live the way I want to some of the time?*

We parted ways.

It wasn't long before Mom came back to the (lovely peach) room my sisters and I shared. "Honey," she began, "I was very wrong to get angry and be impatient with you. There's no excuse for my sin, and I'm very sorry. Will you please forgive me?"

Our quarrels often ended this way. If I had a dollar for every time my mom was the first to admit her sin and ask my forgiveness, I'd . . . well, I'd do a lot of things. Mom's humility melted my proud heart. I felt sorry for how selfish I had been. "I was wrong too, Mom, for not serving you and the rest of the family," I said. "Will you forgive me for disobeying and leaving such a mess this morning?"

She forgave me freely, but I knew we had more to talk about. Mom always turned our conflicts into opportunities for both of us to examine our hearts. After analyzing her own motives and inviting me to evaluate her actions, she would help me to look at my heart. So she asked me questions such as: "Why is it that you leave everything so disorganized?" and "Have you stopped to consider how your harried morning routine inconveniences the family?" and "What do you think you want more than to glorify God and serve others in this situation?"

Clearly the problem was my prideful independence and selfishness. I loved to do things my own way. I wanted to leave my room a mess, without someone telling me to clean it up. I didn't care how it affected my family. It was these wrong desires that sparked the conflict with my mom.

Perhaps you've had an argument with your mom or daughter today. Maybe you even had one yesterday and the day before that. Maybe you fight all the time. Or it could be that you clash only once in a while, but when you do, boy, is it a blow-up! Or possibly your relationship is marked by constant tension and unspoken bitterness. It's like the elephant in the living room that no one talks about. Or you may be a mother-daughter pair who only experience relatively minor and infrequent clashes. But no matter your conflict variation, you feel lost in a jungle of disagreements.

Sinful mothers and sinful daughters living together in a sinful world means that conflict is inevitable. You may have noticed that many of our conflicts occur right within our own families, and consequently we sin against the people we love the most. Theologian John Stott points out that because of the Fall, family relationships are tainted by sin: "For the family life which God created at the beginning and pronounced to be 'good' was spoiled by human rebellion and selfishness. Relationships fell apart. Society was fractured."[1]

But there is good news. It doesn't have to *stay* this way. By God's amazing grace, we can resolve any argument, regardless of how severe it has become or how long it has lasted. James 4 shows us a clear path out of the jungle of conflict. To guide us through these verses, I'm going to borrow my dad's sermon notes. Besides being a great dad, he's been a pastor for many years; so he has a lot more wisdom than I do. His message— "Cravings and Conflict"—has completely revolutionized the way I think about and work through conflict.[2] (Thanks, Dad!)

Let's begin by reading James 4:1-2: "What causes quarrels and what causes fights among you? Is it not this, that your passions are at war within you? You desire and do not have, so you murder. You covet and cannot obtain, so you fight and quarrel."

Dad points out three truths:

1. Conflict is worse than we think.
2. Conflict is simpler than we think.
3. Conflict is easier to resolve than we think.

Let's start with the bad news: *Conflict is worse than we think.* I doubt that many of us consider our mother-daughter conflict to be as serious as it really is. For example, have you ever employed one of the following phrases to describe your relationship?

❀ We just don't get along.
❀ We have issues.
❀ We're wired differently.
❀ Our personalities clash.
❀ We have different preferences.
❀ We don't see things the same way.

If we're honest, I'm sure we'd all have to admit to using phrases such as these to brush aside our disagreements. But God uses stronger terms than "personality clash" or "differing preferences" to depict our conflict. He uses words such as *coveting* and *war* and *murder*. Our anger and quarrelling and nasty words are to God as serious as if we were at war with each other. He even compares them to murder. How sobering.

The situation appears even more grim when we realize that our conflict isn't simply a disagreement between mother and daughter. When we quarrel and fight, we are disobeying God. We are rebelling against His great command to love one another. We are despising His Word that says, "the anger of man does not produce the righteousness that God requires" (James 1:20). Only when we agree with God, that our sin against each other is also sin against Him, can we make progress toward resolving our conflicts.

But though serious, our conflicts are also *simpler than we think*. I know it doesn't always *feel* that way. Conflicts can seem complicated. For example, have you ever been smack in the middle of a fight, only to forget what you were mad about in the first place? I certainly have. And sometimes conflict hits you out of nowhere. One minute you're chatting amicably, and the next thing you know, you're in a heated argument. What just happened? Then there is the recurring conflict, the one you could set your clock by. You know it's coming, but you can't seem to get out of its way. And so it happens over and over and over again.

Scripture exposes conflicts for the simpletons they really are. In answer to the question: "What causes quarrels and what causes fights among you?" God responds with a rhetorical question of His own: "Is it not this, that your passions are at war within you? You desire and do not have" (James 4:1-2). Inside the freight train of every conflict is one powerful engine: a sinful desire for something that we want but don't get. Another word for this sinful desire is a craving. Counselor David Powlison remarks, "Cravings underlie conflicts."[3]

Conflicts don't create the problem. They reveal the problem. They expose the sinful cravings lurking in our hearts. When we don't get what we crave, we quarrel and fight. It's that simple. And this truth—that cravings underlie conflicts— is the key to resolving even the most complicated mother-daughter disagreements.

Take your most recent conflict, for example. What did you crave that you weren't getting? Did you want to be left alone, be understood, have your own way, or be in control? Was it that you weren't getting the appreciation, recognition, or affirmation you thought you deserved? Or maybe you didn't want to clean your room, take care of your siblings, or do whatever it was your mom told you to do. Perhaps you longed to get even, inflict hurt, be right, or win the argument.

At first glance, many of these desires don't seem like a big deal. But when we are willing to fight in order to get them, it's a sure sign they are a bigger deal than we think. They have developed into sinful cravings. As Dr. Powlison (paraphrasing John Calvin) writes: "The evil in our desires often lies not in what we want but that we want it too much."[4]

Our own evil desires—and not the other person's—must be our first and chief concern. God reminds us in James 4 that the root cause of conflict is the "passions that are at war within *you*" (emphasis added). Not the other person, but you. So if we point our finger before repenting of our own sinful cravings, we've strayed from the path that leads out of Conflict Jungle.

Moms, may I encourage you to set a godly example by being the first to ask forgiveness for your sinful cravings? Take it from a daughter—the swiftest way to your daughter's heart begins with humility. Paul Tripp says it plainly: "Here is a good rule: Deal with yourself before you deal with your teenager (Matt. 7:3-5)."[5] But, girls, let's not sit back and wait on Mom. Let's race to see who will be the first to repent of sinful desires. Why? Because it's a race to win for the glory of God. And now that we understand how simple conflict really is, nothing should hold us back.

Conflict is also *easier to resolve than we think*. There is a way out of the brutal cycle of mother-daughter disagreements. We *can* step off this wearying treadmill and proceed in a God-glorifying direction together. James 4:10 records the solution to conflict: "Humble yourselves before the Lord, and he will exalt you."

That's it. No exception clause. No writing 100 times on the

blackboard: "I will not fight again." No penance. It's that easy. We simply need to humble ourselves before God and confess our sins to Him and to our mother or daughter.

But as my dad says, "It can only be this easy because our Savior has done the unimaginably difficult." Jesus died on the cross, crushed by the weight of our sinful conflicts. He bore the wrath of God that we deserved for our fighting and quarrelling. Because of Jesus' work on the cross, we can humble ourselves, repent from our evil desires, and be reconciled to God and to each other. Scripture invites all who are in conflict: "Let the wicked forsake his way, and the unrighteous man his thoughts; let him return to the LORD, that he may have compassion on him, and to our God, for he will abundantly pardon" (Isa. 55:7). Resolving conflict is easy because Jesus Christ has already done the incredibly hard work on the cross.

So the next time you find yourself in the midst of a mother-daughter argument, remember that James 4 points the way out of Conflict Jungle. Your conflict is worse than you think, simpler than you think, and easier to resolve than you think. Mothers and daughters who quickly and consistently work to resolve their conflicts will be best equipped to pass on the language of biblical womanhood.

For Further Study

❀ *The Peacemaker: A Biblical Guide to Resolving Personal Conflict* by Ken Sande

❀ "Cravings and Conflict," audio message by C. J. Mahaney, available at www.sovereigngraceministries.org.

A Mother's Faith

by Carolyn

So tell me about your family," the man said, turning his attention to me. C. J. and I were having breakfast with a prominent Christian leader. "How old are your daughters, did you say?" "Six, ten, and eleven," I replied. "Ah," he said, leaning back in his chair with a smile. "Those are delightful ages. They still think Mommy and Daddy are the most wonderful people in the world. But all that changes when the teenage years come."

My breakfast—not to mention my day—was spoiled. That sense of dread at the approach of my daughters' teenage years, always nipping at the edges of my imagination, played out once again in panoramic view: the little hints of trouble, the minor instances of disobedience—where would it all lead? *Nicole has been disrespectful lately. Is this the first sign of full-fledged rebellion? Sometimes Kristin is so quiet. Will she become more withdrawn? Janelle's mischievous streak could mean real trouble in a few years. Things will probably get worse and worse, and soon my daughters won't even like me anymore. What can I do to stop this from happening?*

"What are your daughters' names?" The benign question jolted me back to reality. I managed to stammer a response, and the conversation moved on. But the gnawing feeling in my stomach remained.

Everything I'd ever heard about parenting teenagers was negative and alarming. This man, although well-intentioned, had only confirmed these fears in my mind. Our culture simply assumes that the teenage years are a time of rebellion against parental authority, as if biological change triggers an inevitable sinful reaction. But as respected author Elisabeth Elliot points out, it wasn't always this way. She says of herself and her siblings:

> We never were *teenagers*. I can't help being very thankful that the term had not been thought of in my day. I think it spared us some silliness and some real pain. It has become an accepted label for a stage in life usually dreaded by parents and relished by children as a time when anything goes. But this is an invention of modern times and affluent societies. . . . We were not taught to expect a stage of chaos and rebellion. Some prophecies are self-fulfilling. If they're never heard, they never happen.[1]

Tedd Tripp, author of *Shepherding a Child's Heart,* is of the same opinion. He writes:

> Most books written about teenagers presume rebellion or at least testing the limits of parental control. My assumption is the opposite. My assumption is that you have carried out your parenting task with integrity and that your children, in the words of Titus 1:6, "are not open to the charge of being wild and disobedient."[2]

The ghosts of my mothering future never materialized. I don't mean to say that there weren't difficulties to work through and challenges to overcome. But, by God's mercy, strife and upheaval didn't overshadow the whole of my daughters' teenage experience. Nicole, Kristin, Janelle, and I only grew closer during their teenage years, and the all-out rebellion I had braced for didn't erupt. However, perplexing and discouraging moments inevitably arrived, and far too often I responded in fear.

Several years ago C. J. and I, along with Nicole and Janelle

(Kristin was living in Chicago at the time), were interviewed at a parents' meeting at our church. The moderator asked C. J. and me, "If you could parent your daughters all over again, what would you do differently?" It was not a tough question. While I am aware of numerous ways I would want to be a better mom, one thing stands out far ahead of the rest.

I wish I had trusted God more.

For every fearful peek into the future, I wish I had looked to Christ instead. For each imaginary trouble conjured up, I wish I had recalled the specific, unfailing faithfulness of God. In place of dismay and dread, I wish I had exhibited hope and joy. I wish I had approached mothering like the preacher Charles Spurgeon approached his job: "forecasting victory, not foreboding defeat."[3]

What mothering failures have you predicted lately? What fears about your daughter lurk around the edges of your mind? Do you assume that your relationship with your daughter will only get worse? Are you anxious about your responsibility to teach her the language of biblical womanhood?

As women, aren't we all vulnerable to fear, worry, and anxiety? And few areas tempt us more than mothering. But *faith* must dictate our mothering, not fear. Faith, as it says in Hebrews, is the "assurance of things hoped for, the conviction of things not seen" (Heb. 11:1).

Faith toward God is the foundation of effective mothering. Did you catch that? Here it is again: *Faith toward God is the foundation of effective mothering.* Success as a mother doesn't begin with hard work or sound principles or consistent discipline (as necessary as these are). It begins with God: His character, His faithfulness, His promises, His sovereignty. And as our understanding of these truths increases, so will our faith for mothering. You see, it is relatively easy to implement new practices in parenting. But if our practices (no matter how useful) aren't motivated by faith, they will be fruitless.

The Bible says that without faith it is impossible to please God (Heb. 11:6). Fear is sin. And as my husband has often graciously reminded me—God is not sympathetic to my unbelief. Why? Because fear, worry, and unbelief say to God that we don't really believe He is "merciful and gracious, slow to anger and abounding in steadfast love and faithfulness" (Ps. 86:15). We are calling God a liar.

Even in the most trying situations with our daughters, we have much more incentive to trust than to fear, much more cause for peace and joy than despair. That's because, as Christians, we have the hope of the gospel.

The gospel begins with some bad news. It confirms the fact that we are *all* sinful, rebellious creatures. Rebellion is not unique to modern teenagers. In Psalm 51, King David laments, "Behold, I was brought forth in iniquity, and in sin did my mother conceive me" (v. 5).

But the gospel doesn't leave us with bad news. The message of the gospel is that Jesus Christ has come to save rebellious sinners: mothers *and* daughters. He lived a perfect, rebellion-free life, fully submitted to His Father, and died a cruel death as our substitute. Then He rose from the dead and is seated now at the right hand of God, the Father.

The truth of Christ's life, death, and resurrection is our hope as mothers. The power of the gospel means that teenage rebellion is not inevitable. Tedd Tripp concurs:

> You have reason for hope as parents who desire to see your children have faith. The hope is in the power of the gospel. The gospel is suited to the human condition. The gospel is attractive. God has already shown great mercy to your children. He has given them a place of rich privilege. He has placed them in a home where they have heard His truth. They have seen the transforming power of grace in the lives of His people. Your prayer and expectation is that the gospel will overcome their resistance as it has yours.[4]

The gospel message should provide us with tremendous heart-strengthening, soul-encouraging hope: Jesus Christ is "mighty to save" (Isa. 63:1). This should kindle zeal to share the truth of the gospel with our daughters. (You will find a simple gospel presentation, "How Good Are You?" in Appendix C.)

Perhaps your home is a place of peace and tranquility, your fears as insignificant as gnats to swat away. Or maybe trials are washing over you like relentless waves. Your anxieties are consuming and overwhelming. They rob you of sleep and plague your waking hours. But no matter the size or the shape of your fears, may I encourage you to take them to the foot of the cross? The gospel isn't an out-of-date message; it is the good news of a saving God who is "a very present help in trouble" (Ps. 46:1). So repent from worry and put your trust in the glorious gospel.

My husband has a Charles Spurgeon quotation as his screensaver, which we would do well to have running across the screen of our minds: "As for His failing you, never dream of it—hate the thought. The God who has been sufficient until now, should be trusted to the end."[5] So let our mothering forecast be one of victory and not of defeat. We have the hope of the gospel in our souls.

For Further Study

❀ *Trusting God: Even When Life Hurts* by Jerry Bridges

❀ *The Cross Centered Life: Keeping the Gospel the Main Thing* by C. J. Mahaney

❀ *Christ Our Mediator: Finding Passion at the Cross* by C. J. Mahaney

A Mother's Example

by Carolyn

Don't you *ever* do that again!" Janelle scolded Patty-Lynn in the severest tone her sweet, little voice could muster. Patty-Lynn (or Lynn-Patty as she was also known) was her Cabbage Patch doll. I listened from around the corner as the reprimand continued in an angry voice: "How many times do I have to tell you that it is not acceptable to disobey Mommy? I am very, very upset with you. That was your last warning, and now you will have to be punished. Do you hear me?"

I was poised to storm the room and nab her for unkind speech, but a single thought halted my well-timed raid: "She's imitating me!" My daughter was only copying an earlier performance of mine when I'd angrily corrected her for emptying out the linen closet. If she was guilty, then I would first have to "arrest" myself.

Children are consummate mimics. They effortlessly take in our accents, mannerisms, and oft-used phrases, making them an indelible part of their personality. They copy the way we hold our purses, talk on the telephone, walk down the street, or put on our makeup. What mother hasn't had the "I want to sink through the floor" experience of hearing her careless words repeated verbatim to an unintended audience?

But more than our traits and style, our daughters also absorb our character. From their earliest years, our behavior is their standard and guide. Our influence, for good or bad, will follow them into the teenage years and throughout their lives. So when they are in a conflict, do they lash out in anger, or do they seek to be peacemakers? When trials threaten to knock them down, who or what do they lean on? How earnestly do they seek the face of God? In all these things, our example will influence their conduct.

If truly understood, the impact of our example should bring us to our knees. Elisabeth Elliot soberly considers the fact that "the example of parents, for good or ill, is an influence far more profound than can be measured."[1]

An authentic godly example is indispensable to the transfer of the language of biblical womanhood. Not only will our model of a godly woman provide a pattern for our daughters to copy, but every virtue we will teach stands or falls by our example. Our example must precede our instruction.

Appropriately did J. C. Ryle warn: "[Your children] will seldom learn habits which they see you despise, or walk in paths in which you do not walk yourself. [She] that preaches to [her] children what [she] does not practice, is working a work that never goes forward."[2]

Paul Tripp points out that if we talk about Christ's love and the Bible but live selfish, angry, materialistic lives, then we are saying with our example that God's truth is only a facade. He writes: "Our teenagers will tend to dismiss or despise the very Gospel we say is of paramount importance. They will tend to reject the God we have so poorly represented, and they, too, will end up serving the idols of the surrounding culture."[3]

While a poor example will dishonor the gospel, the godly example of a mother is among the most profound forces in human history. We read in the Bible of the mother-daughter pair, Lois and Eunice, who shaped the life of Timothy. In a survey of church history we are introduced to the influential mothers of great Christian leaders such as Augustine, Charles Spurgeon, and John and Charles Wesley—men whose love for the gospel resulted in thousands coming to know Christ.

Two hundred years ago John Angell James, in his book titled *Female Piety*, reported on the effect of a mother's example in his day:

> At a pastoral conference, held not long since, at which about one hundred and twenty American clergymen, united in the bonds of a common faith, were assembled, each was invited to state the human instrumentality to which, under the Divine blessing, he attributed a change of heart. How many of these, think you, gave the honour of it to their mother? Of one hundred and twenty, above one hundred! Here then are facts, which are only selected from myriads of others, to prove a mother's power, and to demonstrate at the same time her responsibility.[4]

Now if the thought of this grave responsibility to be a godly example enervates your soul, you are not alone. When we compare our shortcomings to our hopes for a daughter's character, the disparity is often conspicuous. If you are like me, you are painfully aware of your imperfection. But this is good, for it brings us back to the cross.

We are sinful mothers; however, we must not forget that the Savior died for sinners such as we. We will never be able to hold up for our daughters a perfect example; however, we should display the humble, honest example of a woman striving after the qualities of biblical womanhood by the grace of God.

In fact, our sins provide an opportunity for the light of the gospel to shine into our mother-daughter relationships. If we humble ourselves, confess our sins, and ask for our daughters' forgiveness, we will be showing the power of Christ's saving work.

I vividly remember one interaction between Nicole and Kristin when they were little. I had gotten angry with Kristin, and afterwards I overheard Nicole reassuring her sister from vast experience: "Don't worry, Kristin—Mom always asks forgiveness." I didn't know whether to be pleased or discouraged.

While I didn't want to believe Nicole had so many illustrations to draw from, I was relieved that her experience, though not of a perfect mom, was at least tempered by some measure of humility on my part.

Paul Tripp concurs: "Living consistently with the faith does not mean living perfectly, but living in a way that reveals that God and his Word are the most important things to you. Such a [mother] can even honor God in [her] failure, with [her] humility in confession and [her] determination to change."[5] Humility isn't just a component of a good example: It's godliness in its purest form.

This truth should give us renewed hope in difficult situations with our daughters. Humility is a powerful tool that breaks down barriers that correction and advice can't on their own chip away. A humble spirit helps us get behind the walls our daughters may erect. It's a doorway into their hearts, no matter how hard they have become.

From the time our girls were old enough to communicate, C. J. and I asked them regularly, "If there is one thing about Daddy and Mommy you could change, what would it be?" Often they said silly things like, "Give me more ice cream." But occasionally their comments provided valuable insight into our deficiencies as parents. And although the phrasing matured over the years, we never stopped asking this question. Why not ask your daughter the same question before the week comes to a close?

Only after we humble ourselves can we encourage our children to follow our example. Comments like "Why don't you do what I say?" or "When will you ever learn?" will not promote the language of biblical womanhood. But our humility will soften their hearts and inspire them to imitate our example of these virtues.

In conclusion, we must not hesitate to encourage our daughters to follow our example. Many mothers consider such a statement prideful. They simply hope their *quiet* example will produce the intended effect. By the grace of God, it may. But we would be wise to emulate the apostle Paul's more aggressive approach. In humility, he encouraged the believers to follow his example as he followed Christ. He exhorted them in 1 Corinthians 11:1: "Be imitators of me, as I am of Christ." And again in Philippians 3:17: "Brothers, join in imitating me, and keep your eyes on those who walk according to the example you have in us." So let's take our daughters by the hand and say, "Come, follow me into the riches of the gospel of Jesus Christ."

A Mother's Love

by Carolyn

O ne of the biggest complaints about motherhood," wrote humor writer Erma Bombeck, "is the lack of training. We all come to it armed only with a phone number for a diaper service, a polaroid camera, a hotline to the pediatrician, and an innocence with the life span of fifteen minutes."[1] In her book *Motherhood: The Second Oldest Profession,* she asserts, " . . . education is the answer. If we only knew what to do and how to do it, we could survive."[2]

Although motherhood as an institution has existed for millennia, I have yet to meet a mother who really thinks she's mastered the trade. We all stumble along, making the same mistakes, on a desperate search for tips, solutions, and sound principles. Then our daughters become teenagers, and we can despair of ever succeeding as a mother—much less passing on the language of biblical womanhood.

But if we would only avail ourselves of holy Scripture, we would find the wisdom and direction we so desperately seek. We must not neglect God's Word while we pan for the fools' gold of worldly counsel.

In Titus 2 we find a genuine nugget of mothering wisdom. It tells us to "love [our] children" (v. 4) tenderly. This may not appear to be a new and novel parenting tip, but J. C. Ryle insisted that this biblical principle is "one grand secret of successful training."[3]

Now I know you love your daughter. You would die for her, and sometimes you feel as if you already have, many times over. You've endured labor and delivery or the innumerable hurdles of the adoption process, only to wake up multiple times per night to feed your little girl. You've changed her diapers, potty trained her, taught her to dress herself, helped her with schoolwork, prepared her three meals a day, washed and ironed her clothes, and driven so many cumulative carpooling hours that your car feels more like your home than your house does. You're a mom, and moms are good at sacrificial love. It's an essential aspect of mothering. But the love Titus 2 is talking about is a *tender* love. It's the warm, affectionate, nurturing kind. It speaks of enjoyment and delight in our relationship with our daughters.

J. C. Ryle described tender love as "a willingness to enter into childish troubles, a readiness to take part in childish joys,—these are the cords by which a child may be led most easily,—these are the clues you must follow if you would find the way to [her] heart."[4] Similarly, Paul Tripp encourages us as parents to "remember what it was like to live in the scary world of the teen years."[5]

A simple test of the effectiveness of tender love requires only a moment of self-reflection. Don't we all respond better to a person who takes an interest in us and expresses affection than to someone who tries to force or manipulate us to comply with their wishes? Our daughters are no different. Discipline, correction, and training are ineffective and even detrimental when void of tender love. But these same tools are more readily welcomed if they come with a kind and gentle hand. The biblical maxim to treat others as you would like to be treated most certainly applies here.

And wasn't it a tender love that the Savior showed to us when He granted us salvation? He leads us with "cords of kindness" (Hos. 11:4), and "He does not deal with us according to our sins" (Ps. 103:10). So the most important reason to apply tender love is because it displays Christ's love to our daughters.

There are countless avenues for us to express a tender love specifically, constantly, creatively, and sincerely. The following are merely seven practical suggestions:[6]

Pray. A godly mother's prayers have "great power" (James 5:16), and so who better to pray for our daughters than us? No one knows them the way we do. No one is more familiar with the unique temptations and pressures they face every day. No one can pray for them with keener insight or greater compassion. We should be committed to loving our daughters by faithfully praying for them. And what's more, we should *inform* them of our prayers. As Charles Spurgeon once said, "No man can do me a truer kindness in this world than to pray for me."[7]

Take an interest. Make it a point to discover your daughter's hobbies and leisure pursuits. Talk to her about them, and learn to share in her enthusiasm. You may even go a step further and participate with her in her favorite activities. For example, my daughter Kristin developed a love for the art of cooking. So I arranged for us to take some gourmet cooking classes offered by the county. This provided a meaningful experience for the two of us to share, and it was a tangible way to express my tender love for Kristin. "Taking an interest" need not require financial expense, but it does call for a heart of love and enthusiasm for the things your daughter enjoys.

Listen closely. Attentive listening entails an eagerness to hear *everything* with regard to our daughters' thoughts, feelings, and experiences. It's more than just keeping our mouths shut. Listening means making full eye contact, not looking around with a blank stare. We don't interrupt, yawn, or prematurely formulate an answer. Careful listening will encourage our daughters to bare their souls to us and share their innermost thoughts. So may our daughters know that we want to hear all about it!

Encourage, encourage, encourage. Proverbs gives abundant proof that encouraging words refresh our daughters' souls: "Gracious words are like a honeycomb, sweetness to the soul" (16:24); "A good word makes him [or your daughter] glad"

(12:25); and "a gentle tongue is a tree of life" (15:4). Let's ask ourselves: Are the words our daughters hear from us primarily condemning and corrective or positive and uplifting? Do our words give them life and make them glad? While correction is necessary at times, our daughters should be the *constant* recipients of our encouragement.

And this encouragement can come in many forms and for many reasons. We can write a note, send an e-mail, encourage them in front of someone else, or simply tell them of our love. We can point out their personality traits and unique talents that we appreciate. We can draw attention to ways they have grown in their passion for God or one of the virtues of biblical womanhood; we can remind them of God's help in the midst of difficult situations. These are all examples of what my husband calls "Evidences of God's Grace"—ways God is at work in our daughters' lives. We must not let a day go by without communicating these encouraging thoughts to them.

Express affection. We should lavish affection on our daughters from the moment they wake up until they go to bed at night. We can do this verbally by simply saying, "I love you," many times a day. We can express physical affection through hugs and kisses. In the midst of correction we should reaffirm our love, reminding them that we discipline them because we love them. We never want our daughters to have even a moment's doubt about our love.

Make memories. One of my favorite ways to express tender love for my daughters was to plan special outings and find unique ways to make memories. Today we have a whole collection of memories that we review often with fondness and laughter. Both the planned activities and the spontaneous moments can all be potential memories if we apply a little creativity. And don't forget to throw in a surprise or two. Everybody loves a surprise! If you're not sure how to get started making memories with your daughter, we've provided a list of our favorites in Appendix D.

These ideas have been just a sampling of the endless ways we can express tender love. Ultimately, our love will make our friendship and our home a safe harbor for our daughters. Tedd Tripp points out:

> The most powerful way to keep your children from being attracted by the offers of camaraderie with the wicked is to make home an attractive place to be.
>
> Young people do not run from places where they are loved and know unconditional acceptance. They do not run away from homes where there are solid relationships. They do not run from homes in which the family is planning activities and doing exciting things.[8]

Let's be the kind of warm and affectionate mothers with whom our daughters want to spend time. Tender love liberally scatters gospel seeds in our daughters' lives. We can trust God to cause these seeds to take root and grow into a mature love for Him.

A Mother's Discipline

by Carolyn

It wasn't an easy decision, but it was time to pull Kristin out of school. The year before, after being homeschooled for three years, Kristin had begged C. J. and me to let her attend a local private Christian school. We agreed, under one condition: She was to be a difference-maker. But Kristin had not kept up her end of the deal.

Outwardly she was a "good" kid, even an exemplary one. She wasn't deceptive or openly rebellious. She worked hard at school and didn't hang out with the wrong crowd. She did all the "right" things. Yet she remained silent when she should have graciously confronted the ungodliness of her classmates. She was tolerant of sin in her own life and the lives of others. We didn't observe a passion for God. She also failed to show consistent love for home and family, one of the foremost characteristics of biblical womanhood. Though subtle, these were serious concerns.

I knew Kristin wouldn't be happy about our decision to homeschool her again. I knew she might resent us. It was tempting to give her what she wanted in order to avoid a potential conflict and retain her affection. But in reality we had no choice. We knew that God was not pleased with Kristin's lukewarm attitude. So C. J. and I deemed it necessary to take action. As parents, we had a deep sense of our responsibility before God to lead, train, and discipline our children for the purpose of holiness. We were bound to the commitment we had made even before our children were born that, "as for me and my house, we will serve the LORD" (Josh. 24:15). (I don't intend to imply here that parents are biblically required to homeschool a lukewarm child. This was simply the option we believed to be most beneficial for our daughter's spiritual growth at that particular time.)

All parents are bound to the command in Ephesians 6:4 to "bring [our children] up in the discipline and instruction of the Lord." While this verse is addressed to fathers, Scripture is clear that a mother's participation is equally significant (Prov. 1:8; 6:20; 31:26; Eph. 6:1; Col. 3:20).

Pastor John MacArthur explains that the word *discipline* in Ephesians 6 means "enforced conformity of the heart and the life to God and His truth."[1] *Discipline* is a strong word that implies deliberate and committed action on the part of parents. It insists that we go to whatever lengths are required to deter our children from sin and to instead direct them in paths of righteousness. My husband used to express his resolve to obey this command by telling our daughters, "If necessary, I will throw my body in front of you to prevent you from sinning."

C. J.'s statement might sound extreme; however, I believe it is biblical. Given the seriousness of sin before a holy God, we as parents must seek to restrain our children from bringing reproach to God's name and pain to others—not to mention sparing them the bitter consequences. We must make every effort to train our daughters and redirect them toward a lifestyle that brings glory to God and that aligns with His Word. Ultimately, our desire is for our daughters to experience the blessings and favor that flow from a life of obedience to God.

Our biblical charge to discipline our daughters means that we cannot be passive parents. We must not think that we are helpless or without recourse to deal with our daughters' sin. Neither turning a blind eye nor remaining ignorant are acceptable options. We cannot afford to assume "this is just a phase" or "this is normal for her age." And we must not subscribe to the theory that allowing our daughters to experience the world will make them stronger. Effective discipline requires more than reactive parenting, which only swings into gear when a crisis hits.

Left to themselves, our daughters will not naturally conform to the Word of God. The truth is that we *all* go our own way apart from the intervention of the Holy Spirit and the correction of godly friends. (This fact should help us guard against self-righteousness.) And if we ignore, minimize, or are at ease with the discrepancies between our daughters' behavior and God's standard, there may be dire consequences.

That's why J. C. Ryle strongly warned parents:

> Beware of that miserable delusion into which some have fallen,—that parents can do nothing for their children, that you must leave them alone, wait for grace, and sit still. These persons . . . desire much, and have nothing. And the devil rejoices to see such reasoning, just as he always does over anything which seems to excuse indolence, or to encourage neglect of means.[2]

Biblical discipline calls for a proactive approach. We must aggressively and intentionally steer our daughters in the ways of the Lord. This idea is illustrated by a television commercial that exhorts parents to oppose teen drug use with the slogan, "Action: The Anti-Drug." We would do well to apply this phrase to our biblical understanding of discipline: "Action: The Anti-Sin." Of course, action alone won't prevent our daughters from sinning. It takes a work of the Holy Spirit, but action is vitally necessary.

However, if our training is to be effective, unity between father and mother is essential. Now unity doesn't mean the absence of disagreement. Differences of opinion are inevitable between couples. What is essential, however, is that we seek to resolve our differences as quickly as possible and present a united front to our daughters. So if you and your husband are not of one mind on discipline, please seek counsel from your pastor or a trusted Christian friend.

To be active in our discipline, we must be watchful, attentive, discerning mothers. We need to study our daughters carefully, ask them probing questions, and maintain a constant awareness of what is going on in their lives. We must be on top of sinful patterns and tendencies (e.g., laziness, self-righteousness, lust, deceit, vanity, pride, and so on). We need to learn their "hot button" temptations.

We aren't simply collecting data on our daughters to file away. We seek to gain insight into their thoughts, temptations, and feelings so we can be poised to bring timely correction, hold our daughters accountable, and set boundaries to protect them from ungodly influences. From there, we want to help our daughters develop a plan to walk in godliness and make progress in biblical womanhood.

However, if our daughters do not show evidence of steady growth in godliness or are unresponsive to our training—dramatic action may be necessary. If a daughter is veering toward worldliness, we may need to cut off ties with an ungodly friend. If she has been dishonest, then maybe we need to remove cell phone or e-mail privileges. Her sin may require measures as drastic as taking away prized privileges or pulling her out of favorite activities. Proactive discipline may mean that you risk upsetting an otherwise "peaceful" situation in your home. It may initiate a conflict or trial. But there is too much at stake not to take action. We want our daughters to reap the sweet fruit of repentance.

But this dramatic action must be accompanied by explanation. Few things are more frustrating to a young person than the "because I said so" answer. This response is appropriate for the small child who does not yet have the capacity to understand our decisions. However, a teenager capable of rational thinking (most of the time!) will greatly benefit from an explanation. Effective mothering involves teaching our daughters to understand from Scripture why we've made particular decisions.

For this reason, C. J. and I had a long talk with Kristin about school, followed by several more conversations. As I had expected, she wasn't happy about our decision. We listened patiently to all of her objections and appeals and answered all of her questions. But then we carefully and thoroughly explained our reasons for bringing her home—our concern for her soul and our love for her. We told her that we wanted her life to bring glory to God and that sometimes that meant we had to make decisions she did not like. We outlined for Kristin the changes we hoped to see from her in the forthcoming year, and we concluded by reaffirming our love and affection for her. Although Kristin didn't agree with our decision, she was confident that we did it for her good. We didn't lose her heart.

If, after you have done all you can, your daughter remains unresponsive to your leadership, may I encourage you to obtain the help of godly friends or pastors? My daughters knew that if they refused to respond to C. J. and me, we wouldn't hesitate to ask others to counsel them. Nicole, Kristin, and Janelle have since told us that this was an incentive to repent. We must not be too proud to position our daughters to receive all the help they need. And in addition to requesting counsel for our daughters, we should seek evaluation of our parenting as well.

The mother of famous nineteenth-century pastor Charles Spurgeon was an example of a woman who aggressively sought to bring her children up in the discipline and instruction of the Lord. Her son wrote of her:

> I cannot tell how much I owe to the solemn words of my good mother. . . . I remember on one occasion her praying thus: "Now, Lord, if my children go on in their sins, it will not be from ignorance that they perish, and my soul must bear a swift witness against them at the day of judgment if they lay not hold of Christ."[3]

May we as mothers all be able to pray as Mrs. Spurgeon prayed. May we be faithful to discipline our children and so help them avoid both the temporary and eternal consequences of sin.

But our discipline must spring from and not be separated from our tender love. In fact, the phrase "bring them up" in Ephesians 6 has a distinct relational component and could be translated "rear them tenderly." We show loving discipline by refraining from harsh or angry correction and by not withholding our affection—regardless of the nature or frequency of our daughters' sins.

Bringing our daughters up in the discipline and instruction of the Lord is hard work. God never said it would be otherwise. But He has promised to provide help and assistance to all who call on His name. This promise gives us the faith and courage to discipline our daughters with the end in view. They may not thank us for it right now. They may not thank us for a long time. But one day they will.

It took some time before Kristin appreciated our decision to take her out of school. But today she is grateful for the consequences she was spared and for the grace she's experienced as a result. And it is so rewarding, as a mom, to observe God's kindness to Kristin. For now she loves the Savior and is devoted to her home and family. As a wife and mother, she selflessly cares for her husband and three small boys. Not only is she a difference-maker in their lives, but she is also seeking to make a difference in other young women's lives. Even her sisters tell Kristin that they want to be like her when they grow up.

The book of James closes with this stunning promise: "Whoever brings back a sinner from his wandering will save his soul from death and will cover a multitude of sins" (James 5:20). Let's be ready and willing to perform this merciful service for the daughters we love.

For Further Study

❀ *Instruments in the Redeemer's Hands* by Paul David Tripp

A Daughter's Honor

by Nicole

My mom, sisters, and I watched the movie together, all four of us huddled on the same couch. *The Birds* was Dad's idea. He thought it would be funny to see us get scared, and he wasn't disappointed.

Despite the nondescript title, we discovered that *The Birds* is not a *National Geographic* special on the treetop warbler. With 1960s-era special effects, this Hitchcock thriller remains a perfectly chilling tale of maniacal birds that conspire to attack human beings. They swarm schoolchildren, strike when least expected, and peck people to death with their bills. I won't give away the ending, but suffice it to say, it's not happily ever after.

To this day, the sight of birds perched on a telephone wire still makes me wince and walk a little faster. I can't quite convince myself that they aren't secretly plotting my demise. Probably a mild case of ornithophobia—fear of birds (I had to look it up; so don't be too impressed). But as scary as *The Birds* is, there are verses in Scripture I find even more frightening because they aren't from a two-hour spectacle on my TV screen. These verses are deadly serious about God's perspective on how I relate to my mom.

Most of us are familiar with the fifth of the Ten Commandments and the promise it contains: "Honor your father and your mother, that your days may be long in the land that the LORD your God is giving you" (Ex. 20:12). But keep reading past Exodus, and you'll find that there are some pretty severe consequences for the sons or daughters who dishonor their parents. A brief sampling is enough to make me shiver:

> *Leviticus 20:9: For anyone who curses his father or his mother shall surely be put to death; he has cursed his father or his mother; his blood is upon him.*

> *Proverbs 20:20: If one curses [or dishonors; it is the same word] his father or his mother, his lamp will be put out in utter darkness.*

> *Proverbs 30:17: The eye that mocks a father and scorns to obey a mother will be picked out by the ravens of the valley and eaten by the vultures.*

Not looking good for the disrespectful daughter, is it? But God is not finished yet. The Bible also says that when we fail to honor our moms, it's as serious as dishonoring God *Himself.* Charles Bridges, author of a commentary on the book of Proverbs, explained, "The cursing of a parent was visited with the same punishment as the blaspheming of God; so near does the one sin approach to the other. The rebel against his parent is ready to 'stretch out his hand against God' himself. (Job 15:25)"[1] These verses frighten me because I have been guilty of dishonoring my mom.

Dishonor comes in many different forms: from open defiance to sly disrespectful comments. For me, it was at some point in my teen years that I began to develop a haughty attitude toward Mom. I grew to think quite highly of my own abilities and opinions and not so highly of hers. I found fault with her clothing, her way of speaking, and the godly priorities of her life. My sin was small in my own eyes, but not in God's. For even one of these "small," proud thoughts I deserve the full punishment of a dishonoring daughter.

I'm not what you would call subtle; so it wasn't long before

Mom perceived my disrespect (days, weeks maybe—I'm so glad it wasn't much longer). She confronted my puffed-up thoughts and pointed out the arrogance and pride from which they sprang. She proved her mother's love for me in spite of my insulting attitude toward her. And God used her kind response to produce sorrow and repentance in my heart.

To set the record straight: Ask anyone who knows my mom, and that person will confirm that I was mistaken in my thinking. Mom is clearly superior to me in every way—beauty, intelligence, gifting, and most importantly, godly character. (She wants me to take this sentence out, but I'm not listening.) But you know, sin distorts and mangles our view so that we no longer see things rightly. I certainly didn't.

To this day I feel sorrow over how Mom must have felt when she uncovered the truth of my haughty attitude. No mother should ever have to experience disrespect from her daughter— least of all, my mother. But even more grievous is the fact that my dishonor was ultimately against God.

So what did it look like to begin honoring my mom? What does honor look like for all of us? Puritan pastor and author Matthew Henry wrote that honor is "an inward esteem . . . outwardly expressed upon all occasions."[2] Honor begins in our hearts and our thoughts. It means that we cherish, esteem, and look up to the woman God has chosen to be our mom. Then we follow through on that attitude by showing respect through our words and our obedience. The scope of honor for our mothers, as the Bible describes it, is far reaching. It includes:

- ❀ Obedience while under her authority (Eph. 6:1; Col. 3:20).
- ❀ Dependence upon her wisdom and counsel (Prov. 6:20-23).
- ❀ Eagerness to receive her training and instruction, especially in the language of biblical womanhood (Titus 2:4-5).
- ❀ Dedication to serving her and meeting her practical needs (1 Tim. 5:4).
- ❀ Respect and esteem for her godly example (Prov. 31:28-31; Eph. 6:1).

❦ Pursuit of a God-glorifying lifestyle that brings her joy (Prov. 10:1; 15:20; 23:24-25).

❦ Encouragement and gratefulness for her sacrifice (Prov. 31:28-31).

(For those of you reading this chapter whose mom is not a Christian or is an immature believer, honor will look different in your case. Though there are many things you can apply from this list, you are not to follow your mom into sin, condone her wrong behavior, or respect her ungodly lifestyle.)

Still not getting the picture of what it means to honor your mom? Well, try this. Stop and think of a person you really admire or wish you could be like. It's probably the first person that popped into your head. Now what kind of thoughts do you have about this individual? Are they admiring thoughts? What kinds of things do you say to him or her (if you get a chance)? Are they flattering and encouraging, sweet and kind? And how do you act toward this person? Do you go out of your way to be around this person, to do things for him or her, to get him or her to like you? If so, you are honoring this individual. We all honor someone, don't we? Well, God commands that we treat our moms this way. And if your mom is already the person you admire—way to go! Honoring your mom is one way to honor God Himself.

There are no "buts" to this command. We shouldn't think we are the exception to this rule. The Bible doesn't say, "Oh, by the way, if your mom isn't cool, or if you don't agree with her decisions, you can disregard this command." The requirement to honor our mothers applies to everyone, all the time, and for the rest of our lives.

God demands nothing less than perfect honor toward our moms. However, maybe you, like me, are guilty of dishonoring your mom, and ultimately God. And you, like me, realize you deserve the awful fate assigned to the dishonoring daughter. It is good for us to begin to comprehend the seriousness of our sin. However, we must not despair: God has provided a remedy for every girl who has dishonored her mother. He sent His Son, Jesus, to earth. Jesus lived a perfect life, including flawless honor of His mother. Yet He received the punishment from God for *our* dishonoring so that we could be forgiven. If we repent and trust in Him, we can be cleansed from our sin. And we can also have hope that, by His power at work in us, we can become young women who honor their moms.

By God's grace the rewards of honor are more wonderful than the consequences of dishonor are scary. We are reminded in Ephesians 6:2-3 that the charge to honor our mother is "the first commandment with a promise, '*that it may go well with you and that you may live long in the land.*'"

The secret of the good life is right here in God's Word: Honor your mom (and dad). Then it will go well with you, and you will receive the favor of God. Who would not want a long and happy life? I don't know who, in their right mind, would turn down an offer like that. Sign me up!

A Daughter's Obedience

by Nicole

Has your mom ever told you to do something that was the *last* thing in the world you wanted to do? My sister Janelle can relate. It happened when she was in the ninth grade.

She was hanging out with some friends. They had all recently returned from the youth group summer mission trip the week before. As they talked, some of the kids began to speak critically about a pastor in the church. The most outspoken was a guy named Mike.

When Janelle told Mom about Mike's slander, Mom insisted that she go back and ask him to apologize to the group for his comments. Listening to slander, Mom said, was by God's standard the same as doing it yourself. Besides, slander is like poison in a church.

Janelle *really* didn't want to confront Mike, but Mom wasn't asking her. She was telling her. So Janelle called him.

Mike took it okay. He didn't see what the big deal was, but he said he was wrong, and he was sorry. The whole thing was over in less than five minutes. Janelle tried not to worry about what he thought of her now. What mattered was that she had obeyed her parents.

Ephesians 6:1-2 backed Mom up in this situation. It says, "Children, obey your parents in the Lord, for this is right. 'Honor your father and mother.'"

Honor and obedience are inseparable. In fact, you honor your mom *by* obeying her. And as much as you might want to find a loophole, there is none here in Ephesians 6:1-2. Obey your parents. In the Lord. This is right. When we were little, my parents taught us to obey "immediately, completely, and willingly." This about sums it up.

But obedience isn't measured by mere outward compliance with the rules. Do you remember the Pharisees—those uppity guys in the Bible who thought they were so holy because technically they kept the law? Well, Jesus exposed them for the hypocrites they really were. He rebuked them: "For you clean the outside of the cup and the plate, but inside they are full of greed and self-indulgence" (Matt. 23:25). Imagine drinking out of a cup that had never been cleaned on the inside. Yuk! Worse, Jesus compared them to whitewashed tombs—attractive on the outside but with a decaying body hidden inside.

These illustrations were Jesus' way of telling the Pharisees that their outward conformity didn't cut it. That was simply a show. Their superficial actions weren't true obedience because true obedience comes from the heart. Likewise, we're only modern Pharisees if we do all the right things, but our hearts are not in it. That's not to say that we wait until we feel like it to obey. But simply doing what we are told is not enough. Genuine obedience isn't measured by politeness to elders, a facade of compliance, or statements about our love for God. True obedience starts in the heart.

To develop a heart of obedience, we must first understand that *God* has put our parents in charge. Parental authority isn't a conspiracy of society to oppress children everywhere. It isn't an outdated, repressive, backward idea. And it isn't a scheme of our parents just to keep us under their thumbs. In fact, our parents haven't even been given an option. They've been ordered by God to lovingly act on His behalf to guide us in His ways.

So when we obey our parents, we are obeying God. And when we disobey our parents (unless they ask us to sin), we are disobeying God. It's that simple. There is a direct link between our attitude toward our parents' authority and our attitude toward God's authority. Obedience to our parents isn't an "us versus them" issue. It's an "us versus God" issue. That raises the stakes considerably, to say the least. Not only does our disobedience take on a whole new level of seriousness, but our obedience becomes that much more important. It not only pleases our parents, but it is pleasing to God Himself. Obedience is all about God.

When we take this in—that *God* has set up Mom's authority—it also gives us faith for her wisdom. (In keeping with our mother-daughter theme, we will focus on obedience to Mom in this chapter. However, we trust it goes without saying that this command applies with Dad as well.) You see, as daughters, we often think we're the ones with all the smarts and that Mom doesn't really know what she's doing. This common malady is called pride. Paul Tripp makes this observation:

> Most teenagers simply don't have a hunger for wisdom. In fact, most think they are much wiser than they actually are, and they mistakenly believe that their parents have little practical insight to offer. They tend to think that their parents "don't really understand" or are "pretty much out of it." Yet most teenagers sorely lack wisdom and desperately need loving, biblical, and faithfully dispensed correction.[1]

Let's face the facts. We young women are seriously lacking in the wisdom department. This should cause us to be humble. It should also transform our perspective of our mother's authority. She probably knows a lot more than we think she does. In fact, she's been endowed with wisdom from God to lead us in His ways. So we should get excited about obedience! Obedience is thrilling because through our mom we can get wisdom and guidance from God. Pretty radical stuff, this obedience, isn't it?

And faith for Mom's authority affects our response when we don't agree with her decisions or even if she makes a mistake. Of course, we are never to obey her if she tells us to sin. (If you and your parents are not in agreement as to whether their counsel is biblical or wise, we encourage you to seek help from a pastor together.) However, most often it's that we *don't want* to do something she requires, or we *want* to do something she forbids. We tend to think Mom is ruining our life, or at least our chances for fun by withholding her permission. Or we worry that obeying her will result in an unfavorable outcome for us.

In Janelle's case, she worried that in confronting Mike she would lose his friendship and approval. But faith for Mom's wisdom and authority made all the difference for Janelle. And faith for *your* mom's authority can make that difference for you too. Because you know that God has established your parents' authority, you can have every confidence that He will honor your obedience and cause all things to work for your good. "For those who love God all things work together for good" (Rom. 8:28).

In fact, obedience is all about good stuff. God didn't establish our mom's authority to make our lives miserable. He put her in charge so we could receive the joy, peace, protection, and happiness that come from walking in God's ways and doing His will. Obedience keeps us within what Tedd Tripp calls the "circle of great blessing."[2] There is security in obedience because we know that God's ways are perfectly safe. There is joy and peace because we know that He Himself is guiding us, and we are happy because we are pleasing God.

These blessings are ours if we choose to live a life of obedience. In Deuteronomy 28, after giving many commands to the Israelites, God takes fourteen verses to lay out the immense blessings of obedience. Here is a sampling:

> And if you faithfully obey the voice of the LORD your God, being careful to do all his commandments that I command you today . . . all these blessings shall come upon you and overtake you. . . . Blessed shall you be in the city, and blessed shall you be in the field. . . . Blessed shall you be when you come in, and blessed shall

you be when you go out. . . . The LORD will command the blessing
on you . . . in all that you undertake. . . . And the LORD will make
you abound in prosperity. . . . The LORD will open to you his good
treasury, the heavens, to give the rain to your land in its season and
to bless all the work of your hands. . . . And the LORD will make you
the head and not the tail, and you shall only go up and not down, if
you obey the commandments of the LORD your God, which I com-
mand you today, being careful to do them. . . . (Deut. 28:1-14)

Wow! God's blessings for obedience are nothing short of spectacular!

Yet each time we choose to disobey, we are essentially toss-ing these blessings in the trash can. "No thanks," we say. "I would rather have my own way than experience the goodness of God." By rejecting God's blessings, we may be thinking that independence is more fun or that true freedom is doing what we want to do. But those ideas are only illusions. Pastor and author John Piper vividly illustrates this point when he writes:

There are sensations of unbounded independence that are not true freedom because they deny truth and are destined for calamity. For example, two women may jump from an airplane and experience the thrilling freedom of free-falling. But there is a difference: one is encumbered by a parachute on her back and the other is free from this burden. Which person is most free? The one without the parachute feels free—even freer, since she does not feel the constraints of the parachute straps. But she is not truly free. She is in bondage to the force of gravity and to the deception that all is well because she feels unencumbered. This false sense of freedom is in fact bondage to calamity which is sure to happen after a fleeting moment of pleasure.[3]

Disobedience to authority isn't true freedom but rather a dangerous choice with inevitable consequences. After describing the blessings of obedience in Deuteronomy 28:1-14, God spells out the consequences for His people if they do not obey His com-mands (vv. 15-68). If the many blessings did not convince you that obedience is a good idea, I would encourage you to read the rest of Deuteronomy 28. The alternative is terrible.

We all deserve these consequences, for who of us hasn't disobeyed? Yet once again we see the marvelous mercy of God: His Son took all the punishment for our disobedience. What's more, by His Spirit, we can now choose to obey: "Therefore, my beloved, as you have always obeyed, so now . . . work out your own salvation with fear and trembling, for it is God who works in you, both to will and to work for his good pleasure" (Phil. 2:12-13).

Janelle didn't see at first how obeying Mom and confronting Mike would result in blessing. But she found out recently. You see, Mike and Janelle were married on June 1 of 2003.

Mike still remembers Janelle's phone call that day, and now he is so grateful that she pointed out his sin. Today he is a young man with a passion for God and a love for his local church. In fact, he serves as a pastoral intern. Janelle's submission to parental authority and her courage to confront made him realize that she was the kind of woman he wanted to marry (not to mention that he thought she was very pretty!).

Now this doesn't mean that the next time you confront a guy, he's the one you're going to marry. But I guarantee that God's blessings will be no less lavish on your life when you choose to obey your mom.

PART TWO

Biblical Womanhood in the Real World

ſowing in ſpringtime

by Nicole

All this mother-daughter talk has been leading somewhere. Somewhere exciting. For the last twelve chapters we've sought to bring you—a mother and a daughter—closer to each other. We've encouraged communication, urged conflict resolution, and informed you of your motherhood responsibilities and daughterly obligations. We earnestly hope that your relationship is stronger and your conversation sweeter than ever before. But happy mother-daughter relationships are only the beginning.

Now it's time to learn about our mission: *to pass on the language of biblical womanhood.* We're not moving on from the mother-daughter relationship. Rather, we're preparing to launch into a whole new level of mother-daughter effectiveness for the gospel.

We're off to discover how the qualities of biblical womanhood play out in the real world of a young woman's life. And if "all the world's a stage," then, Mom, think of yourself as your daughter's director. We've attempted to provide a script, and now it's up to you to help your daughter, not to act it out, but to truly live out the language of biblical womanhood. The following nine chapters are written *to* your daughter; however, they are for you, Mom, to help her understand and apply. We encourage you to read them along with her and use the questions in Appendix A to talk about what you've read.

I must say here that the following chapters don't pretend to be a comprehensive discipleship manual for mothers and daughters. If they were, we would be examining vital topics such as the study of God's Word, spiritual disciplines, and much more. (In "A Word to Fathers" at the back of this book, my dad has provided several book recommendations to get your daughter started on a more comprehensive study of God's Word.) Rather, we have a very specific aim: to equip mothers to train their daughters to display the feminine qualities of biblical womanhood.

But first, girls, let me talk straight with you for a minute. I realize you may be a little skeptical about this "biblical womanhood" idea. Perhaps you assume it's a meaningless term, the kind you cram into your head the night before a test only to drag and drop into the "trash can" icon of your brain at 3 P. M. the next afternoon.

Or maybe you think that biblical womanhood is an archaic concept or an old-fashioned idea. Not true. It has everything to do with *your* life as a young woman in the twenty-first century.

Biblical womanhood is important if you're confused and uncertain about your future and what to do with your life. It matters, say, if you've ever agonized over your physical appearance—your weight or a perceived flaw. Biblical womanhood is relevant when you have a crush on a guy. It helps you if your girlfriends have turned their backs on you. It's indispensable when the crowd you hang with is pressuring you to do something you know is wrong. Biblical womanhood even has something to say about the clothes you choose to wear. Simply put, if you're still breathing, then biblical womanhood is essential for you. To discover how a godly young woman responds to these and many other situations, you need only to study this unique language. Biblical womanhood is God's design, His blueprint for women, young and old. And there is no area of your life that these qualities do not touch.

I warn you that if you grab hold of these qualities, you will find every part of your life transformed. You might not even recognize yourself when the ride is over. And don't think for a moment you can put biblical womanhood on the shelf and pick it up again in a few years. These qualities aren't just for your mom or a married woman with babies. Biblical womanhood applies right here, right now, today.

You have a precious opportunity, one that many older women wish they could have back again. You only have it for a short time before it will be lost forever. You have the chance, as a young woman, to invest today in biblical womanhood and to collect the benefits for the rest of your life.

Today's choices determine what tomorrow will be for you. Your decisions this moment will influence the direction of your entire life. So *now* is the time to seek with all your heart to develop the qualities of biblical womanhood.

John Angell James, a Puritan pastor, exhorted young women:

> But remember, my young female friends, and the lesson cannot be too deeply impressed upon your minds, that the seeds of woman's life-long excellences must be sown in the springtime of existence; and it must be done in part by her own hand, when aided and taught by others to prepare the soil. The flowers of womanly excellence, which she would wish to grow in her future character, must be previously and carefully selected, and be contemplated and anticipated by her in all their full-blown beauty and their richest fragrance, even while she is yet in youth.[1]

Now you have the option to squander these precious years trying to be the most popular girl in school, which probably won't happen (and even if it does, it won't mean anything the day after graduation). You can devote yourself to good grades or civic excellence. But these too are of little value compared with biblical womanhood. You might even be content to do as little as possible and thus gain even less.

Or you can choose to join other young women who are passionate about the beauty of biblical womanhood, women whose first language is *girl talk*, who, together with their moms, are living now for what counts tomorrow and in eternity.

In conclusion, let me remind you of the primary reason we are so excited, zealous, and even a little crazy about biblical womanhood. The reason is the gospel. The language of biblical womanhood radiates the good news of Jesus Christ. It sets a girl apart from the worldly culture around her because she displays qualities only possible through the grace of God. For it is God's grace alone that trains us "to renounce ungodliness and worldly passions, and to live self-controlled, upright, and godly lives in the present age" (Titus 2:12).

It's impossible for people *not* to notice the girl who speaks the language of biblical womanhood. And so in this way she will "adorn the doctrine of God our Savior" (Titus 2:10). So don't waste another moment. Take Mr. James's advice and, with the help of your mom, sow the seeds of biblical womanhood in the springtime of your life. The choice is yours.

It's a Girl!

by Carolyn

For young women to understand biblical womanhood, they must first appreciate what it means to be a woman—by God's definition. To discover the meaning of femininity, we must, in the words of Fraulein Maria, the nanny-turned-mommy in *The Sound of Music*, "Start at the very beginning, a very good place to start." We must peer back in time to the inauguration of womanhood when God created our great, great, great, great . . . grandmother, Eve.

The origin of the first woman is recorded in elegantly simple language in Genesis 2:21-22; 1:27:

> *So the LORD God caused a deep sleep to fall upon the man, and while he slept took one of his ribs and closed up its place with flesh. And the rib that the LORD God had taken from the man he made into a woman and brought her to the man. . . . So God created man in his own image, in the image of God he created him; male and female he created them.*

Woman was the beautiful handiwork of God, our Creator. She was God's idea. In fact, of all God's brilliant creation production, man and woman together were the finishing designs, the final act.

The important point here is that *God* created us. We are the planned and foreordained determination of an all-wise, all-powerful, and all-loving God. It is not mere chance that we are female; our gender is not accidental. We were intentionally and purposefully created.

When God created the first woman and every woman thereafter, He made fully feminine creatures. You and I did not become feminine because our moms gave us dolls and put pink dresses on us. We were born feminine because we were *created* feminine.

Some people in our culture put forth the notion that femininity is a matter of cultural conditioning. They argue that the only essential difference between men and women is our anatomy, that any other perceived differences are only the result of upbringing, education, and social influences.

But Genesis teaches otherwise. Because God created male and female, women are different from men. We are innately feminine with certain divinely intended qualities that make us unique. Granted, we can enhance our femininity or detract from it, but we cannot change it. Our sex chromosomes are in every cell of our bodies. Our femininity is a fact. It's also a gift of grace from a loving God.

We can't look to our culture to find our feminine identity; we can't consult our feelings to discover how to live according to our feminine design. Everything that we are and everything that we do must be rooted in God's plan. Our identity as His creation determines everything for us as women.

Now I know we promised you that biblical womanhood would be exciting—and it is! Learning about God's creation of us as women may not seem very relevant to your life at this point, but hang on. Because we must first understand who God made us to be in order to know how we are supposed to act. As one godly and astute woman, Elisabeth Elliot, once said, "The fact that I am a woman does not make me a different kind of Christian, but the fact that I am a Christian does make me a different kind of woman."[1]

We know from reading God's Word that we as women have

a certain role and function consistent with our unique design. So what is our unique feminine purpose?

Again our answer is waiting for us in the creation story. In Genesis 1:28 God assigned both male and female to fill and subdue the earth. Then in chapter 2 He gave the details of how this assignment is to be fulfilled. Men and women were assigned different and yet equally important functions as fellow stewards of creation.

Adam was created first, signifying his role as leader and initiator. God gave him the tasks of working and caring for the garden and naming the animals. But then in Genesis 2:18 God declared that there was something amiss in all the stunning perfection of the garden: "Then the LORD God said, 'It is not good that the man should be alone; I will make him a helper fit for him.'"

God created the first woman, Eve, and assigned her the honorable task of *helper*. As a fully feminine creature, she was stamped with a helper design. She was created both complementary to and yet distinctly different from man. She was created equal in worth and yet different in function.

Now because you have grown up in a feminist-soaked culture, the idea of being a helper might sound demeaning to some of you. You may be thinking: *I'm not anyone's helper. I am better than that.* But being a helper does *not* mean that woman is inferior to or less significant than man.

The Bible is crystal clear on this point: Men and women are equal in worth and importance. Remember Genesis 1:27: "So God created man in his own image, in the image of God he created him; *male and female he created them.*" Men and women were both created in the image of God. Both are equal in value and dignity. We simply have different functions, which are equally honorable and significant.

Confident in the truth that we are of equal worth in God's sight, we are free to fulfill our feminine design. We are free to express our innate feminine characteristics given to us by God.

For both the order in which woman was created and the helper function we have been assigned have implications for how we live our lives and how we relate to others.

Now in this little chapter, we are only able to scratch the surface of biblical femininity—its importance and its application. Entire books have been written on this vast topic. We want to highly recommend *Recovering Biblical Manhood & Womanhood*, edited by John Piper and Wayne Grudem. This book is a thorough work of vast significance.

But here we simply want to introduce you to biblical femininity and give you an idea how—with the help of your mom—you can apply it. To help us understand what this looks like, Jeff Purswell, dean of the Sovereign Grace Ministries Pastors College, offers the following definition: "Biblical femininity suggests an inner disposition that is supportive, responsive, and nurturing in its various roles, responsibilities, and relationships."[2]

This definition is not exhaustive, as Mr. Purswell is quick to point out. Neither is it a narrowly defined set of behaviors. Rather, drawing from a broad range of scriptural ideas, it identifies certain characteristics that represent the *disposition* of femininity. And your helper design isn't something you cash in come marriage. For you were born feminine, remember? Your helper role is called for today.

Let's inspect our feminine character more closely and consider how we display it in everyday life. First, we note that biblical femininity is *supportive*. Jeff Purswell expands on the meaning of this word as "an inclination towards giving help and assistance."[3] This aspect of femininity appears at the very creation of woman as a "helper suitable" for man (Gen. 2:18).

As women, we have been specially equipped to provide strategic, effective, and valuable help and aid to those around us. We are God's handpicked support staff for creation. When we operate and serve in a supportive role, we will experience the joy of fulfilling God's design.

So take a moment to consider, with the counsel of your mom, whom God would have you assist and support during this season of your life. Maybe it's your mom who could use practical help in the home. Maybe your parents could benefit from your skills or labor on behalf of their business. No doubt there are numerous ways you can support the efforts of your church to further the gospel. Possibly you know a mom with young children who would be blessed to have you lend a hand in her home. Or you can use baby-sitting money or your allowance to financially support an impoverished child.

As you can tell, the opportunities to help and assist others are limitless. And, as my husband loves to remind the people he serves with, "all this simply wouldn't be possible without your help!" What godly endeavor can you support and "make possible" today?

But there's yet another facet to our helper design: We are called to be *responsive*. Jeff Purswell defines this as "an inclination to cooperate with and respond to appropriate leadership structures."[4] There isn't much mystery here. God has set up authority figures in our lives for our good. For married women Scripture is clear that "the husband is the head of the wife" (Eph. 5:23), and this is to guide how the wife relates to her husband. But this aspect of femininity is not limited to married women, since we all should display an appropriate attitude toward proper authorities in our lives. First and foremost are parents, then godly pastors, teachers, and the governing authorities.

Spend a moment in self-evaluation. How well do you cooperate with and respond to the authority God has placed over you? When your dad or mom instructs you, are you eager to obey, or resentful and defiant? Do you enthusiastically encourage and follow your pastor, or are you critical and ungrateful? When teachers give assignments, do you grumble and gripe, or do you thank them?

Do you see how expressing our femininity, speaking the language of biblical womanhood defies all worldly expectations of young people? What a golden opportunity you have to reflect the gospel by living true to your helper design!

Keep this in mind as we consider the final aspect of our feminine identity: our inner disposition toward *nurturing*. Mr. Purswell speaks of this quality as "an inclination to provide care and strength to others."[5]

In Scripture nurturing is highlighted in verses that praise a woman's care for her family (Prov. 31:27-28) and that encourage women to orient themselves to the needs of the home (Titus 2:3-5). This expression of our femininity is perhaps the most easily recognizable. Who can deny that as women we have been outfitted to excel at comfort and care? No doubt you have countless memories of receiving comfort and care from your mom. God has created us with a heightened sensitivity to the needs and pain of others and a large capacity to express compassion.

However, as with all these aspects of our helper design, we can either enhance this quality or tear it down. We must be faithful to cultivate our God-given nurturing bent. Our efforts to care for others are also a one-of-a-kind expression of the love of Christ.

We don't have to look far for a chance to nurture others. Children, of course, are the most obvious people with whom to start. If you have siblings, you can begin with them. If not, then "borrow" some by seeking to show tenderness to children around you. Baby-sitting is a great way to get started. When my girls were little, there were young women who served C. J. and me by baby-sitting or just taking the girls out to have fun. Years later my girls were able to return the favor and baby-sit for their children.

Serving in a nursing home, showing kindness when someone is sick, or caring for your grandparents are all ways to be nurturing. But this trait extends beyond the practical to the spiritual. Every time we reach out to a lonely girl, encourage another person, pray for someone or share a word of Scripture, we are providing strength for someone's soul.

The avenues to express our helper design are exciting and boundless! They will also take different expressions in your various relationships. For instance, come marriage and motherhood, these qualities are to be displayed very specifically in relation to your husband and children. But although femininity may look a little different for a teenage girl or a single woman than for a married woman, we are called to fully express our helper design, no matter what our age or marital status is. In fact, the following chapters will be full of ways that you can nurture and be responsive and supportive in the everyday situations of your teenage life.

As we follow God's pattern for our lives and cultivate and embrace our helper design—fulfillment, joy, and the assurance that "this is right" will inevitably result. As theologian Wayne Grudem remarks, "God intended it to be fun to be a man and woman and to enjoy the way that He made us!"[6] So let's have some fun—God's way. Let's get started on a lifetime of expressing our God-designed femininity.

For Further Study

❀ *Recovering Biblical Manhood & Womanhood,* edited by John Piper and Wayne Grudem
❀ *What's the Difference?: Manhood and Womanhood Defined According to the Bible* by John Piper
❀ *The True Woman* by Susan Hunt
❀ *Let Me Be a Woman* by Elisabeth Elliot
❀ *Feminine Appeal: Seven Virtues of a Godly Wife and Mother* by Carolyn Mahaney

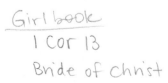

Girl book
1 Cor 13
Bride of Christ

Foolish Fans and the Fear of God

by Nicole

The football stadium rippled with screaming students, including Janelle and her friends. They were celebrating the victory of our hometown favorite, the University of Maryland. This last win of the season secured Maryland's spot in the illustrious Orange Bowl for the first time in many years. In a burst of foolish excitement, students poured out of their seats and rushed the field. So did Janelle's friends.

As they streamed away, someone yelled back, "C'mon, Janelle." She shook her head and stood rooted to the aluminum bleachers as if she'd stepped in chewing gum with both feet.

While she appeared resolute, a battle was raging inside. She knew it was illegal to rush the field. But, on the other hand, *It can't be that bad if everyone else is doing it. What if they think I'm self-righteous—or not any fun? They may get annoyed with me and not want to hang out anymore.* Janelle looked around to see if any friends had stayed behind. Only one guy with a hurt leg remained.

If you've been in junior high or high school more than five minutes, you've probably faced a similar situation. Here's the scenario: Everyone (or an important someone) wants you to do something that you know is wrong, and you have a choice—to go with the crowd or do what's right. Maybe they're gossiping or making fun of someone or using profanity. You have to decide whether to participate, remain silent, or stand up for the truth. Maybe it's the immodest clothing or the ungodly music they're playing. Or they could be actively recruiting you to have sex, smoke, or steal.

Whatever it is, the urge to do what others are doing can feel irresistible. The fear of what will happen if we don't is sometimes paralyzing. So we may try to convince ourselves that following the crowd is no big deal.

This compelling desire is commonly referred to as peer pressure. But the Bible calls it the "fear of man," or in this case maybe the fear of teenagers. The fear of man has two faces. On one side it is a fear or dread of risking someone's disapproval or rejection. But flip it over, and it looks like an aggressive campaign to be popular and get attention.

The fear of man is a slip-n-slide straight to sinful behavior. The Bible warns us that the "fear of man lays a snare" (Prov. 29:25). It sets a trap, and we are all in serious danger of falling into it. We may do many foolish, ungodly things because we want others to like us, include us, or make us feel important and accepted.

That's why some people think it's impossible for young women to make it through the teenage years without engaging in ungodly behavior. The peer pressure, they say, is just too strong to resist. But the Bible loudly says, "THAT'S NOT TRUE!" It insists that it *is* possible to escape the snare of the fear of man and to walk the way of biblical womanhood (1 Cor. 10:13).

So what protects us from giving into this fear?

It's what kept Janelle in those bleachers that night. It wasn't strawberry Bubblicious on her tennis shoes. It was *the fear of the Lord*. She was aware that God was watching. And Janelle's fear of Him was stronger than her desire to impress her friends. You see, when we truly know God, our fear of Him will overrule our desires for the approval of others. We will long for His approval most of all.

The fear of the Lord is not only our protection from the fear of man, but it is also the unique mark of the godly woman. It's the one sure way to tell her apart from all others. As Proverbs tells us, "Charm is deceitful, and beauty is vain, but *a woman who fears the* LORD *is to be praised*" (31:30).

What is the fear of the Lord? As author Jerry Bridges admits, "It's better described than defined."[1] So let me tell you about the girl who fears the Lord.

She's the girl who knows her God:

❀ She experiences a profound sense of awe at the thought of God, the creator of the universe who is "sitting upon a throne, high and lifted up" (Isa. 6:1).

❀ She trembles with dread and wonder before the perfect, pure, and holy Lord of all "who will by no means clear the guilty" (Ex. 34:7).

❀ She marvels at the undeserving love and mercy of Jesus Christ who "is slow to anger and abounding in steadfast love, forgiving iniquity and transgression" (Num. 14:18).

❀ She delights in the perfect wisdom of God, the beauty and order of His universe, the unfathomable perfection of His plan of salvation, and His loving supervision of every detail of her life.

Her awe of God results in obedience to Him:

❀ She seeks the Lord and delights in God's Word (Ps. 1:2).

❀ She hates evil. She doesn't admire those who love it (Prov. 8:13). That's why she doesn't flirt with a guy or lie to her parents or cheat on a test or gossip about others or care what people think about her.

❀ She confesses her sin, serves in secret, cultivates inner beauty, humbly embraces God's plan for her life, and trusts Him no matter what.

You recognize her because:

❀ She is full of joy, peace, and hope for the future (Prov. 10:27).

❀ She has a strong confidence (Prov. 14:26), rest and satisfaction (Prov. 19:23), and contentment in God's care and provision (Ps. 34:9).

❀ She's the one to whom God and man give praise (Prov. 31:30-31).

How closely does your profile match that of the godly girl who fears the Lord? Even as I write, I am discouraged by my lack of resemblance. All too often I look like the girl who fears man more than God. I want to fear the Lord and obey Him, but many times I fail.

Maybe you, like me, are discouraged by the lack of the fear of God and the abundance of the fear of man in your life. But we can take hope from Psalm 34:11. There the Lord beckons us: "Come, O children, listen to me; I will teach you the fear of the LORD."

How exciting! God, in His perfect holiness, was once opposed to us because of our sin and fear of man. But through the blood of Jesus He has become our heavenly Father. Now God beckons us to come, sit at His feet, and learn to fear Him.

Gaining the fear of the Lord will not be easy. In fact, if we try to do it on our own, we will certainly fall short. Without God's help it's as absurd as a toddler setting out to climb Mt. Everest. But, the Lord promises, "I will teach you. Take my hand, and I will lead you to the top of the mountain."

Our journey begins with prayer. It's how we respond to God's invitation to come to Him. We shouldn't try to get halfway up the mountain before we ask for His help. We must run straight to Him and cry out: "Teach me your way, O LORD, that I may walk in your truth; unite my heart to fear your name" (Ps. 86:11). If we have a longing to know the fear of the Lord, He will surely teach us.

The Lord also teaches us to fear Him through His Word. As one author describes it, the Bible is like "a textbook on the fear of the Lord."[2] My sister-in-law Megan started nursing school yesterday. She has a stack of thick textbooks that together are almost as tall as I am (in case you're curious, I'm five feet, two inches). They contain the knowledge of the human body that she must know to properly care for her patients. The Bible is our textbook on the most important subject of all: God. If we read it faithfully, we will learn to fear the Lord.

And, of course, the other way to acquire the fear of the Lord is to get help from Mom. This is why the mother-daughter relationship is key to passing on the language of biblical womanhood. If you have a godly mother, she can offer a wealth of practical insight on how to apply the fear of the Lord in everyday situations.

Let's make it our resolution (we don't have to wait for January 1) as well as our life's goal to obtain the fear of the Lord. It is the priceless quality of the godly young woman, the means to rise above the fear of man, and the basis for a hopeful future. As it says in Isaiah 33:6 (NIV), "[The Lord] will be the sure foundation for your times, a rich store of salvation and wisdom and knowledge; the fear of the LORD is the key to this treasure."

So why don't you get some hot green tea (like me) or coffee, black (like Mom), and sit down and have a chat together about the fear of the Lord.

For Further Study

❈ *The Joy of Fearing God* by Jerry Bridges
❈ *When People Are Big and God Is Small* by Edward T. Welch

Best Friends

It couldn't have happened at a worse time. Or so I thought. Just as I was turning thirteen, all my friends disappeared. Okay, there were only two of them to begin with. But in my world they equaled everybody. So when they became best friends, and I became odd-girl-out, it was the most difficult thing that had ever happened to me.

Overnight, it seemed, the rules had changed. It wasn't enough anymore to be semi-normal (whatever that is) and the same age as the other girls. Now in order to make and keep friends, I had to be "cool" (whatever *that* is). I had to keep up with the latest clothing trends and hairstyles. I had to learn new slang words never spoken in my home before. I had to be up on all the latest music and movies and gossip. And about the only thing I got was that I really didn't get it.

Losing my friends meant I had no one to talk to at youth group—except the adult leaders (or the boys, but of course they weren't an option). No one to invite me to sleepovers or call me on the phone. No one to send me a card on my birthday. Most humiliating of all, it meant hanging out with my *younger* sister and her friends.

I love my sister Kristin, and I liked her friends, but mooching off your little sister for friends is like shouting to the world: "I'm not cool enough to make any friends of my own!"

Poor Kristin wasn't elated about the idea either, but with some reluctance she included me. (I still owe you one, girl!)

Well, I think you get the awful picture. My carefree life had suddenly sprung a leak, and I was abruptly immersed in the cold, wet reality of life and friends.

The teenage years come with upheaval and change, especially in the friendship department. As girls, we tend to approach these friendships with a lot of emotion. I know I did. We latch onto a new friend and don't let go. We get possessive, easily offended. We can be selfish, petty, and insincere, friendly one day and cold the next. Our friendships are sometimes the source of our greatest joy and at other times the cause of our deepest depression.

But the essential question is: How do we speak the language of biblical womanhood when it comes to friendships?

It probably doesn't surprise you that God has a lot to say about friends. In Ecclesiastes 4:9-10 He declares: "Two are better than one. . . . For if they fall, one will lift up his fellow. But woe to him who is alone when he falls and has not another to lift him up!" What's God saying here? For one, He's telling us that friends aren't optional. They are essential. In other words, you won't find the "Lone Ranger" Christian in the Bible.

It's not simply friends that are a necessity, but *godly* friends. The Bible gets specific about the kind of friends we should have—and whom we should avoid. So what are the essential qualities of the godly young woman's friends? While this is not an exhaustive list, here are some necessary characteristics:

❀ A biblical friend fears the Lord. "I am a companion of all who fear you, of those who keep your precepts" (Ps. 119:63).

❀ A biblical friend encourages. "But exhort one another every day, as long as it is called 'today'" (Heb. 3:13).

❀ A biblical friend corrects. "Better is open rebuke than hidden love. Faithful are the wounds of a friend" (Prov. 27:5-6).

❀ A biblical friend forgives. "Whoever covers an offense seeks love" (Prov. 17:9).

❀ A biblical friend loves. "A friend loves at all times" (Prov. 17:17).

Although I don't know her, I would venture a guess that these qualities describe your mom. Maybe you've never thought of her in the friend category before; she's just Mom. But if you have a godly mom, then maybe it's time to reconsider the ideal friend from a biblical perspective.

I didn't always put my mom in the friends column either, but that all changed when I lost my friends. I discovered that my mom was the best kind of friend I could have. My sisters found the same to be true, but they didn't have to lose all their friends to figure it out!

As we each maneuvered through the teenage years, Mom was our closest confidante, rowdiest cheerleader, wisest advisor, and godliest example. Her guidance and correction kept us from straying into many consequences of worldliness and sin. Her passion for God and encouragement spurred our own love for Christ. She was the most important, influential person in our young lives—our best friend.

While Mom was our best friend, my sisters (and eventually I) also developed friendships with peers who fit the description of the godly friend in Scripture. It is great fun to go through the teenage years with biblical friends our own age. We can spur each other on to know Christ, provoke one another to godly living, serve alongside each other, and make many memories together.

If you don't have godly friends your own age, or even more difficult, if your mom is not a biblical friend to you, remember that we all have one best friend in Jesus. Charles Bridges's words are ever true:

> Let his people bear witness, whether he be not the greatest, best, most loving, most . . . faithful of friends. Truly he "loveth

at all times." He is a friend to them that have no other friend; . . . a friend who abides, when all others have passed away. Mark him as a present friend, known and tried, able to enter into all that most deeply affects us.[1]

The Bible not only lists the attributes of a good friend. It also warns us (especially as young women) against the danger of ungodly friends. It tells us not to hang out with an angry young woman "lest you learn [her] ways" (Prov. 22:24-25) and that "the companion of fools will suffer harm" (Prov. 13:20).

One of the most common excuses we make for choosing ungodly friends is that "they need me to be a good influence." J. C. Ryle reminded young men that "bad company, ruins good morals" (1 Cor. 15:33). He went on to write:

> Good friends are among our greatest blessings;—they may keep us back from much evil, quicken us in our course, speak a word in season, draw us upward, and draw us on. But a bad friend is a positive misfortune, a weight continually dragging us down, and chaining us to earth. Keep company with an irreligious man, and it is more than probable you will in the end become like him. That is the general consequence of all such friendships. The good go down to the bad and the bad do not come up to the good.[2]

So, girls, let's admit the truth: If we hang out with ungodly friends, sooner or later, we will probably be like them instead of the other way around. And starting with our moms, let's pursue some friends who will sway us toward godliness.

It is hard to imagine a greater service that a mom can perform than to keep a close watch on her daughter's friendships. My mom continually monitored the effect our friends had on us and we on them. If a particular friendship produced worldly inclinations, an increase in sinful attitudes, or ungodly behavior, she would pull us back from that relationship. At the same time, Mom intentionally led us to pursue friendships with *godly* young women.

Moms, guarding your daughters' friendships may require deliberate action at times, and it doesn't come without risk. It may mean hard choices concerning whom your daughter spends time with and whom she doesn't—choices that may offend those involved (including the parents of your daughter's friends). And you must be careful to avoid self-righteousness. However, when these decisions are motivated by love, they will not only protect your daughter but serve her friends as well.

My own season of friendlessness was a blessing in disguise. After a year or so, God brought me new friends who loved Him and inspired me to grow in godliness. It was certainly worth a year without friends to end up with friends like that. But best of all was the friendship I forged with my mom—one that only grows stronger as the years go by.

What About Guys?

by Nicole

When did it happen? When did those grubby, annoying, uninteresting, and downright disgusting little boys become the ones we think are so cute, whose attention makes us blush and whose affection we wish to attract? From changing bodies and raging hormones to a whole new world of desires, "guys" are a big issue for girls.

While this is certainly part of the natural order of things—God created us as girls to be attracted to boys (and vice versa)—the fulfillment of these desires is only intended for the marriage relationship. Thus the topic of purity is urgently relevant for every girl who wishes to speak the language of biblical womanhood.

Temptations to impurity are more numerous today than ever before. The enticement of lustful thoughts and the attraction of immoral behavior are encouraged by a constant stream of ungodly messages from our culture.

But God's standard of absolute purity has not changed one bit. He still requires perfect purity in thought, word, and deed. Scripture challenges young women with these poetic, yet solemn words: "Daughters of Jerusalem, I charge you by the gazelles and by the does of the field: Do not arouse or awaken love until it so desires" (Song of Songs 3:5 NIV).

In answer to this call, Titus 2 requires older women to give specific attention to the area of purity as they train the younger women. In her book *Feminine Appeal,* which takes a closer look at Titus 2:3-5, my mom writes that purity means "to be holy, innocent, chaste, not contaminated. This word has to do with sexual propriety, avoiding any immorality in thought, word and action."[1]

Not only is there intense pressure from the world to dispense with purity, but there is also temptation from within. Sin lurks in our hearts, seeking to entice us to lust. Author Kris Lundgaard offers further insight here: "Indwelling sin works like this—enticing, threatening, even bullying. . . . It is powerful even in the lives of believers and . . . it constantly works to press us into its evil mold."[2]

Because of the presence of indwelling sin, God directs us to draw upon His inexhaustible supply of grace so that we can fight sexual temptation and grow in purity. The following, adapted from *Feminine Appeal,* are three weapons we must employ, with God's help, in this battle for our souls.[3]

Set our hearts and minds on things above. It is only through the cross that we obtain freedom from our sin and accomplish our quest for purity. Take note of the deliberate order of Colossians 3:1-5:

> If then you have been raised with Christ, seek the things that are above, where Christ is, seated at the right hand of God. Set your minds on things that are above, not on things that are on earth. For you have died, and your life is hidden with Christ in God. When Christ who is your life appears, then you also will appear with him in glory. Put to death therefore what is earthly in you: sexual immorality, impurity, passion, evil desire, and covetousness, which is idolatry.

Did you catch what comes first? The first step in putting to death sexual immorality, impurity, and evil desire is to seek things that are above. Growth in purity can only be realized as we look upward to Jesus Christ.

Does that mean we minimize or dismiss impurity in our lives? Does this indicate that God is tolerant of evil desire or sexual immorality? Of course not! God neither makes light of nor ignores our sin. He hates sin. That is why Jesus had to die on the cross. Our Savior's death not only secures our forgiveness for sin, but it also demands that we forsake sin and provides us with the power we need to overcome it (Rom. 6:6-7; 2 Cor. 5:14-15).

Let us never forget to put first things first. Our conquest of sin begins with a deliberate resolve to set our hearts and minds on things above. As we contemplate what Christ has done for us, we will be compelled to pursue purity for His glory.

Make no provision for the flesh. You need to find out what history homework is due tomorrow. It's a great excuse to send a text message to Derek, the guy you like at your church's school. He responds quickly with the information and tags on a comment about the upcoming youth meeting Saturday night. This begins a mini "conversation" about the snacks at youth group and a mutual friend who won't be there because she got her wisdom teeth pulled. Two days later Derek finds a reason to send you a text message—also about the youth meeting—and you "chat" again for a little while. Soon it becomes a part of your daily routine to send and receive messages from Derek on your cell phone. You find yourself thinking about him more often and wondering when you'll hear from him next. Soon the messages become more personal and even flirtatious. You feel a little guilty about not telling your mom, but it's nothing serious you tell yourself. You airily dismiss your conscience and send Derek another message.

This scenario I've just described may or may not be a familiar temptation to you. Regardless, Scripture teaches that we *all* have areas where we are susceptible. Now I am not insinuating that text messages to guys are sinful. However, I *am* insisting from God's Word that we never indulge our sinful desires in our relationships with guys.

In Romans 13:14 we read, "Put on the Lord Jesus Christ, and

make no provision for the flesh, to gratify its desires." Or as author and pastor Joshua Harris tells himself, "'Don't pack a lunch for lust.' I must not pamper or provide even a little snack for the lust of my heart to feed on."[4] In response to Romans 13:14, each of us needs to ask, "When, where, and with whom are we most tempted to give into our flesh and gratify its desires?"

Paul told Timothy to "*flee* youthful passions" (2 Tim. 2:22). In 1 Corinthians 6:18, we are exhorted to "*flee* from sexual immorality." This verb *flee* indicates a very strong reaction to temptation. It means to run away or take flight.

It is not enough to simply *walk* away. We are to *run* from temptation as fast as we can. In the case with Derek, that may require you to confess your sin to your mom, stop replying to Derek's text messages, turn off the cell phone, and if necessary, throw it away! We're deceived if we think we're strong enough to handle it. We wouldn't be urged to *flee* temptation if it was something we could manage.

It is crucial that we identify the times, places, people, and sources that can present us with sexual temptation. And we must devise a biblical strategy in order to make *no* provision for our flesh. What's the first step? You guessed it: time to talk to Mom.

Finally, be honest and pursue accountability. Remember Adam and Eve's response after they sinned against God in the Garden of Eden? They hid from Him. They evaded personal responsibility for their disobedience.

Guess what? You and I struggle with the same tendency; we are inclined to hide. Like Adam and Eve, we seek to avoid owning up to our sin. Yet to attempt to hide our sin or escape blame is perilous. We will not grow in purity if we do.

And that is one reason why God has given us our moms. They are our greatest allies in the battle against impurity and lust. Through our relationship with them, we can receive counsel, support, and encouragement in our struggle against sin. So let me implore you to take full advantage of the grace God has provided through your mom in this area. Don't let pride or fear or self-confidence hold you back. Do not hide your sin, but rather honestly confess and ask your mom for help.

In order for your mom to effectively help you come up with a plan to pursue purity, you must get specific. Tell her who, what, where, and when your greatest sources of temptation are. As you humble yourself in this way, God will use your mom's encouragement and correction to help you grow in purity. So open your heart to your mom and invite her to remind you of the gospel — the forgiveness of sin, the cleansing from all impurity, and the power to walk in holiness.

One of my mom's tactics for helping my sisters and me escape impurity was to insist that we avoid foolish conversations with peers about "who likes who" or about sex. Instead, she encouraged us to share our crushes and temptations with her and bring our questions about sex to her.

Mom didn't simply insist we talk to her. She made it easy for us to come. She would periodically quiz us about our latest crush, which prompted us to come out with it. And she never acted shocked or appalled by our confessions. Mom was aware that "no temptation has overtaken you that is not common to man" (1 Cor. 10:13). Her gracious humility and unconditional friendship made her a safe harbor to which we could come and receive help.

When my sisters and I each turned thirteen, my parents gave us a purity ring. The act of receiving and wearing that ring was a pledge—to our parents and ultimately to the Lord—to adhere to God's standard of purity. In turn, Mom and Dad committed to help and support our quest for godliness and purity. I imagine your parents are just as eager to cheer you on and assist you in the same way.

While temptations to lust and impurity *do* abound today, God's standard remains the same, as does His grace to be pure— in thought, word, and action. In addition to the Holy Spirit, God has provided another helper by giving us our moms.

We need not cave into the pressure of the world and our own sinful desires, but we must use all our weapons in this fight. As we set our hearts and minds on things above, make no provision for the flesh, and pursue honesty and accountability, we can prove to the world that, by the grace of God, purity is possible.

For Further Study

❀ *Not Even a Hint: Guarding Your Heart Against Lust* by Joshua Harris

❀ *The Enemy Within: Straight Talk About the Power and Defeat of Sin* by Kris Lundgaard

True Beauty

by Carolyn

It was over thirty years ago, but I still remember it like it was yesterday. Sitting in high school orchestra class with my cello resting between my knees, I was chatting with my classmates while we waited for the orchestra director to arrive. My friend Sally, the violist, was sitting next to me. Bored with waiting, she began examining my hands.

Now I have very long fingers and veins that stick out no matter what I do. For this reason I always disliked my hands. So I remember being mortified as she held her small, pretty hands up to mine and announced loudly, "Your fingers are *so* long!" But that wasn't enough. She also required verification from *everyone* in the class about the extraordinary extra half-inch of fingertip that I possessed. After her comments, my disdain for my hands only grew.

I am sure that I'm not the only high school student who ever fretted over a physical feature she didn't like. Today women and girls alike are taking drastic measures to change their undesirable features. "Extreme Makeover" type reality shows fill the television lineup. It's even become popular for parents to pay for a daughter's plastic surgery or breast augmentation as a graduation present or birthday gift. Anorexia and bulimia are rampant among teenage girls.

The image of beautiful today, says author Jean Kilbourne,

has only become "more tyrannical and more perfect than ever before." A major reason, she says, is "the advent of computer retouching . . . more than retouching, it's a kind of digital altering of the image so that they can now take a model and make a composite woman. The ideal image now is so completely, impossible to achieve."[1] So the models themselves don't even look like their picture. Their "perfect" beauty is an illusion, unattainable. And yet women, young and old, are consumed with trying to achieve that "look."

This zeal for perfection prompts questions: Why? Why are girls (and sometimes their mothers) so obsessed with physical beauty? Why do they go to such radical lengths to be beautiful as defined by *Allure* magazine? Why aren't they pleased with normal?

To differing degrees we have believed that beautiful is better, that physical beauty will bring satisfaction and recognition. You know the promises: If you're beautiful, you will be happy and successful. You will be popular among the girls, and you will be desirable to the boys. You will achieve lasting intimacy and true love. You will be confident and secure. You will be important and significant.

Yet the message is a lie. Physical beauty doesn't deliver as advertised. It doesn't ensure happiness, fulfillment, or success. We can validate this by observing the most physically attractive women in the world. Take for example, Halle Berry. This glamorous actress was "the first African-American to represent America at the Miss World pageant. She has won enough beauty titles to last a lifetime. And she has an Oscar . . . to her credit."[2]

But what does Halle Berry think about her beauty? "Let me tell you something," she has said, "being thought of as a beautiful woman has spared me nothing in life. No heartache, no trouble. Love has been difficult. Beauty is essentially meaningless and it is always transitory."[3]

Our culture puts forth a false standard of beauty and a false message about beauty. But ultimately it's the sin of our hearts that motivates us to believe them. These lies appeal to all the things our hearts desire. We desperately want success, recognition, significance, importance, and approval.

For mothers and daughters, Scripture reveals the falsehood and the futility of the quest for physical beauty. "Charm is deceitful and beauty is vain" (Prov. 31:30). This word *charm* actually means "bodily form." It is perfect form and beauty that our culture esteems and pursues with fervor; yet God exposes this pursuit as sinful. Nowhere in the Bible are women instructed to wish for, ask for, or strive for physical beauty. Neither does the Bible portray physical beauty as a blessing for those who have it.

This is why, in 1 Peter 3:3, we are exhorted: "Do not let your adorning be external—the braiding of hair, the wearing of gold, or the putting on of clothing." Now God is not saying that women shouldn't style their hair or wear jewelry, for then He would also be barring clothing—and we know that is not the case.

However, what the 1 Peter verse is forbidding, says Matthew Henry, is the "inordinate love and excessive use (that is, the abuse) of them." He goes on to say, "we must not set our hearts upon them, nor value ourselves by them, nor think the better of ourselves for them, nor pride ourselves in them, as if they added any real excellence to us."[4]

God is not opposed to us making ourselves beautiful; rather, He unveils in this passage *how* women are to make themselves beautiful. First Peter 3:4-5 tells us to "let your adorning be the hidden person of the heart with the imperishable beauty of a gentle and quiet spirit, which in God's sight is very precious. For this is how the holy women who hoped in God used to adorn themselves."

Now don't despair. A "gentle and quiet spirit" is not referring to a person with a quiet personality. In fact, it is possible for a girl to have a quiet personality and *not* have a gentle and quiet spirit. And it is just as feasible for a girl with an effervescent personality to *have* a gentle and quiet spirit. This spirit is not a personality type.

A gentle and quiet spirit, simply put, is a steadfast peace because of a steadfast trust in God. A girl who possesses a gentle and quiet spirit humbly responds to whatever God chooses for her life, regardless of the cost. Mary, the mother of Jesus, is certainly the best example: "Behold, I am the servant of the Lord; let it be to me according to your word," she said, when the angel informed her she would give birth to the Son of God. She humbly accepted God's will, despite what it cost her. She displayed a steadfast peace because of her steadfast trust in God.

First Peter 3:4-5 doesn't tell us how it works, but when we trust God, we are actually making ourselves beautiful. And not only in God's eyes; this beauty is apparent to others as well. Also instead of fading as our physical attractiveness does (by your late twenties you will already be considered past your prime), we grow more beautiful as we grow older.

The beauty our culture esteems may turn some heads, but the beauty God calls us to cultivate will make a lasting impact. When a cute girl walks by, people notice—guys especially. But that's the end of it. Her beauty makes a fleeting, momentary impression. However, a girl who cultivates inner beauty, who cultivates a steadfast trust in God—*her* beauty will have a lasting effect on the lives she touches.

So which beauty are you going for? Here's a ten-question quiz to help you determine the truth. Spend some time with your mom and answer the following questions:

1. Do I spend more time each day caring for my personal appearance than I do in Bible study, prayer, and worship?

2. Do I spend excessive money on clothes, hair, and makeup, or is it an amount that is God-honoring?

3. Do I want to lose weight to "feel better about myself," or do I desire to be self-disciplined for the glory of God?

4. Am I on a quest for thinness to impress others, or do I seek to cultivate eating habits that honor God?

5. Do I exercise to try to create or maintain a good figure, or do I exercise to strengthen my body for God's service?

6. Is there anything about my appearance that I wish I could change, or am I grateful to God for the way He created me?

7. Am I jealous of the appearance of other girls, or am I truly glad when I observe girls who are more physically attractive than I?

8. Do I covet the wardrobe of others, or do I genuinely rejoice when other girls are able to afford and purchase new clothing?

9. When I attend an activity, do I sinfully compare myself with others, or do I ask God to show me whom to love and how to do it?

10. Do I ever dress immodestly or with the intent of drawing attention to myself, or do I always dress in a manner that pleases God? (We'll talk about modesty in the next chapter.)

If most of your answers were "yes" to the first half of each of these questions, then it's likely you've been sinfully striving after physical beauty to get attention. Why not make a switch and spend your time and energy on a beauty that will never fade? Cultivate a trust in God that will draw attention to the beauty of the gospel. God is eager and willing to help you change.

In the pursuit of true beauty, we need to each acknowledge God's providence and receive with gratefulness the body and appearance He has given us. I know this isn't always easy. As I said at the beginning, I never liked the appearance of my hands—especially after the embarrassing experience in orchestra class. It wasn't until years later that the Holy Spirit was kind enough to use a passage of Scripture to correct my attitude.

I discovered Proverbs 31 where the woman of virtue is described as working with "willing hands" (v. 13). Also "she opens her hand to the poor and reaches out her hands to the needy" (v. 20). I realized my hands weren't merely decorative. They had a kingdom purpose. I saw how sinful (not to mention silly) it was to care about the appearance of my hands instead of my Creator's purpose in making them. God has given me these hands to serve and reach out to others.

Elisabeth Elliot tells how missionary Gladys Aylward learned this important lesson:

> She told how when she was a child she had two great sorrows. One, that while all her friends had beautiful golden hair, hers was black. The other, that while her friends were still growing, she stopped. She was about four feet ten inches tall. But when at last she reached the country to which God had called her to be a missionary, she stood on the wharf in Shanghai and looked around at the people to whom He had called her.
> "Every single one of them," she said, "had *black hair*. And every single one of them had stopped growing when I did. And I said, 'Lord God, *You know what You're doing!*'"[5]

A loving God has determined what we look like. He decided how tall we would be, the color of our eyes, and all the unique features that make up our appearance—right down to our fingers. We can spend the rest of our lives pining about the results of God's determination, or we can receive with gratefulness His design, knowing that He does all things for His glory and our good.

David said, "I praise you, for I am fearfully and wonderfully made" (Ps. 139:14). When was the last time you worshiped God for the way He created your body? Anything less than a heart filled with gratitude and praise to God for our physical appearance is sinful and grieves the Lord.

We must not simply reject the world's view of beauty, but we must also pursue true beauty as defined by the Bible: the inward beauty of the heart. And this beauty has some serious advantages over the world's beauty. It lasts longer, works better, and is pleasing to the one whose opinion matters most. So instead of an extreme body makeover, maybe it's time for an extreme heart makeover. Let's pursue the feminine beauty of a gentle and quiet spirit.

Taking God to the Gap

by Nicole

Girls are always wondering what guys want in a girl. If you're curious about what *godly* young men admire, I've got the inside scoop. Jack and Jason are a couple of young guys who represent countless men committed to glorifying God in their relationships with young ladies.

Before they tell us what they like, let's hear what they *don't* appreciate. You may be surprised.

> Jack: When ladies whom I'm friends with dress immodestly, it definitely has a negative effect on our friendship. When a woman dresses immodestly, it makes it difficult to see her as a sister in Christ. There is a constant battle going on as I'm talking with her. Communication becomes more difficult as I'm trying to listen to her, because I'm also trying to fight temptation.[1]
>
> Jason: When I see girls dressed [in] a suggestive way, I not only turn my head away, but I pray for them. Obviously there is a deeper issue—they are looking for affirmation in the wrong ways. My question is, Is that how you want guys to see you—as a sex object? Or would you rather have a guy know you and care for you because of your character, not just your outward beauty?[2]

What these guys *do* appreciate is a girl who dresses modestly.

Jack: It is such a blessing to have friends who care for us enough to be selfless and to sacrifice what might look attractive in order to help me and other guys with sexual lust. When ladies dress modestly, it's beautiful and makes me want to hang out with them more. I think modesty is so attractive and helpful in friendship because it makes it easier for a friendship to be centered around God and for fellowship to be unhindered.[3]

Jason: I love seeing girls who dress in a way that is [modest]. . . . Even though our culture tells you it's OK to wear clothing that is sexy or almost nonexistent, I want to challenge you to walk a different road. There are plenty of ways to be hip and trendy and to look great without being seductive or flirtatious.[4]

Not only do Jason, Jack, and all godly young men respect and value a modest girl, but most importantly God is pleased with her as well. Modesty is the outward and often the most visible mark of a biblical young woman. It is one of the qualities that God requires of women specifically; so we should pay close attention to our dress. Inspired by the Holy Spirit, Paul writes in 1 Timothy 2:8-10:

I desire then that in every place the men should pray, lifting holy hands without anger or quarreling; likewise also that women should adorn themselves in respectable apparel, with modesty and self-control, not with braided hair and gold or pearls or costly attire, but with what is proper for women who profess godliness—with good works.

Maybe *modesty* is a new word for you. Perhaps you've had a vague idea that it meant "ugly" or "out of style." Before now it never occurred to you that *God* had something to say about the clothes you wear. Well, let's take a closer look at this quality of biblical womanhood and see why it's so important. As my dad likes to say, "Let's take God to the Gap."[5]

Notice in this verse that Paul doesn't say, "Skirts should be such and such a length" and "Blouses must cover such and such amount of skin." He tells the women to dress with "modesty and self-control." Modesty is much more than a dress code; it's about the heart beneath the clothes we wear. Again quoting my dad: "Any biblical discussion of modesty begins by addressing the heart, not the hemline."[6]

You see, immodest dress is more than simply wearing a short skirt or low-cut blouse. Immodesty is an expression of pride and self-importance, the opposite of humility. Revealing, seductive clothes are the costume of a woman seeking to draw attention to herself rather than bring glory to God. So modesty, then, is humility expressed in dress. It is the attire of the godly woman.

Pastor John MacArthur elaborates:

> How does a woman discern the sometimes fine line between proper dress and dressing to be the center of attention? The answer starts in the intent of the heart. A woman should examine her motives and goals for the way she dresses. Is her intent to show the grace and beauty of womanhood? Is it to reveal a humble heart devoted to worshiping God? Or is it to call attention to herself, and flaunt her . . . beauty? Or worse, to attempt to allure men sexually? A woman who focuses on worshiping God will consider carefully how she is dressed because *her heart will dictate her wardrobe and appearance*.[7] (emphasis added)

Our wardrobe is a public statement of our heart motivation. So what kinds of clothes proceed from a humble, modest heart? "Women should adorn themselves in respectable apparel, with modesty and self-control, not with braided hair and gold or pearls or costly attire" (1 Tim. 2:9).

Now adorning ourselves with "respectable apparel" doesn't mean we need to raid our grandmother's closet. Paul is instructing the women to stay away from clothing and accessories that are extravagant, showy, revealing, or sexually enticing. He is encouraging restraint and moderation in dress for the purpose of purity.

Author Nancy Leigh DeMoss recommends two very simple

guidelines. She suggests that while our clothes may be stylish, we must not be guilty of "exposing intimate parts of the body" or "emphasizing private or alluring parts of the body."[8]

Not sure what this means for *your* wardrobe? Then why not spend an afternoon with your mom and go through the "Modesty Heart Check," Appendix E at the back of this book? It might be time for a closet overhaul!

Modesty is of the greatest importance because it honors God. But it also protects our brothers in Christ from sin. Women are sometimes ignorant of the effect of their bodies on the eyes and hearts of men. But, for the most part, if we're honest, we'll admit that we know exactly what we're doing. We enjoy the attention of guys. As a pastor-friend of ours once remarked, "Guys lust and girls want to be lusted after."

While it may seem harmless, this behavior is selfish and unloving toward our brothers in Christ. Instead of seeking to serve them by dressing modestly, we are callously focused on serving ourselves because we relish their attention.

A greater awareness of the temptation to lust that men face should motivate us to help them by the way we dress. With that in mind I want you to hear from another young man, Kevin, about his daily fight for purity:

> Each and every day is a battle—a battle against my sin, a battle against temptation, a battle against my depraved mind. Every morning I have to cry out for mercy, strength, and a renewed conviction to flee youthful lusts. The Spirit is faithful to bring me the renewal I need to prepare me to do war against my sin, yet the temptation still exists.
>
> Sometimes, when I see a girl provocatively dressed, I'll say to myself, "She probably doesn't even know that a hundred and one guys are going to devour her in their minds today. But then again, maybe she does." To be honest, I don't know the truth—the truth of why she chooses to dress the way she does. All I know is that the way she presents herself to the world is bait for my sinful mind to latch onto and I need to avoid it at all costs.[9]

For the sake of Kevin and every other man striving for purity, my parents were committed to raising modest daughters. They educated us about how men are stimulated visually. They examined any article of clothing that came into the house, giving it a thumbs up or sending us straight back to the store with the receipt. I'll admit it was frustrating to spend hours at the mall and have nothing to show for it. There were moments when that frivolous, selfish desire for cool, tight jeans overtook my desire to serve others. That's when Mom and Dad would remind me of the young men who were trying to glorify God. My clothes could either help or hinder them. When they put it like that, I was quickly saddened by my selfishness.

I'm not saying that we are solely to blame for male lust. But as Richard Baxter (writing 400 years ago) so aptly put it:

> You must not lay a stumbling-block in their way, nor blow up the fire of their lust. . . . You must walk among sinful persons, as you would do with a candle among straw or gunpowder; or else you may see the flame which you did not foresee, when it is too late to quench it.[10]

As hazardous as immodesty is, our modest dress has an even greater power to bring glory to God. Paul explains this truth in the very same chapter of 1 Timothy. He introduces the command to modesty with an explanation of the gospel. Paul writes:

> God our Savior . . . desires all people to be saved and to come to the knowledge of the truth. For there is one God, and there is one mediator between God and men, the man Christ Jesus, who gave himself as a ransom for all, which is the testimony given at the proper time (2:3-6).

Our modest clothing can attest to the fact that the gospel has changed our lives. This is why Paul urges us to develop a reputation—not for flaunting our bodies but for good works (1 Tim. 2:10). In the chapters to follow, we will discover the opportunities for good works all around us—in our homes, churches, and communities.

So which do you think about more—shopping or good works? What are you most noticed for—what you wear or your kind deeds? What is most eye-catching about you—your clothing or your character? Why don't we spend some mother-daughter time evaluating our wardrobes and then reach out to others by doing good works?

For Further Study

❀ *The Look: Does God Really Care What I Wear?* by Nancy Leigh DeMoss

❀ "The Soul of Modesty," audio message by C. J. Mahaney, available at www.sovereigngraceministries.org

20

Future Homemakers

by Nicole

As a young woman, I often lay in bed at night and wondered about my future. I stared hard into the darkness, as if God had put the answers there. I had a longing to do great things for God. I imagined myself as a missionary in another country, maybe even a nurse. (I assumed my tendency to faint at the sight of blood would not be a problem.) I had visions of speaking to crowds of women, leading many to the gospel.

What I didn't yet understand was that God's plan for me was greater than what my imagination could conjure up. It was also very different than what I thought.

How about you? What are your dreams and aspirations for your future? How do you answer the well-meaning adults who ask about your plans after high school?

It may surprise you to learn that God in the Bible has already given you a sneak peek into your future. As women, we are all appointed to be keepers of the home (Prov. 31:10-31; 1 Tim. 5:14; Titus 2:5). Someday you may be called to love a husband and bring up children and make a home for them. Or as a single woman, you may be entrusted with a home from which you extend hospitality and vital service to your church and community. While you may pursue many other God-honoring tasks or occupations throughout your lifetime, you are also called to be a homemaker.

This is our purpose in life, what John Angell James calls a "woman's mission,"—to "affect society through the medium of family influence."[1] You see, being feminine isn't just who we are; it's also what we do. Our feminine identity comes with a unique task: to change the world by devoting ourselves to home life.

Now this does not mean that the Bible confines girls and women to their homes. The Proverbs 31 woman—the ideal homemaker—pursued endeavors outside of the home for the good of her family. And, of course, single women will have careers that require them to work beyond the home. But Scripture unapologetically sets forth the high priority of the home for each and every woman.

Although this is our clear mission from God, not many young women aspire to be homemakers these days. While there are many other worthy careers they may consider, homemaking isn't usually on the list of desirable options.

However, it wasn't so long ago that women thought differently about homemaking. As author Danielle Crittenden points out, "Whether it's the pleasure of being a wife or of raising children or of making a home—[these] were, until the day before yesterday, considered the most natural things in the world."[2] Today the most natural thing in the world is for girls to consider any career *except* that of homemaker. So what happened? When did homemaking fall off the radar screen for young women?

To make a very long story short, forty years ago a revolution known as the feminist movement set out to "liberate" our mothers' generation from being tied down to the home. And part and parcel of the feminist message was "a disdain of domesticity and a contempt for housewives."[3]

And there is perhaps no greater measurement of the success of feminism than the fact that our generation no longer considers homemaking a viable career. As my mom has written, "Feminist philosophy has become thoroughly integrated into the values of mainstream society—so much so, that it has been absorbed and applied by the majority of women, even many who do not consider themselves feminist."[4] The feminist revolution is not a revolution anymore; it's simply a way of life.

While motherhood has made a comeback in the ratings of late—and only as a worthy interlude in an otherwise successful career—homemaking in its full scope remains unpopular. Thus you may not have thought of housewives (a term usually employed while looking down on someone) as being world-changers before. But looks can be deceiving. True greatness isn't always flashy or attention-grabbing when it arrives on the scene. I didn't see it at first either.

My mom is a homemaker. I grew up with a living model of a woman who utilized all her intelligence, creativity, and energy to create a home and care for her husband and children. But I didn't always fully appreciate the true significance of her chosen career.

Sure, I wanted to get married and have kids someday and have a home of my own, but I lacked a biblical understanding and vision of the importance and priority of my future calling. However, Mom did not allow me to remain ignorant for long. Through Scripture, hours of conversations, and helpful books, she presented to me the noble calling of a homemaker and its powerful effect in the world.

I learned that, as John Angell James wrote, quoting Adolphe Monod, "The greatest influence on earth whether for good or for evil, is possessed by woman."[5] Modern-day pastor John MacArthur echoes his sentiment:

> The family might survive the problems with children and husband-fathers if the women who are wives and mothers were faithful to their godly calling. Their influence is so strong and pervasive in the home that it can mitigate the other influences. . . . when a wife and mother fulfills her God-given duty, she acts as a barrier against that family's dishonoring God and His Word.[6]

Mom not only taught me of the power of a homemaker's

influence in the world but about the fulfilling nature of her job. Dorothy Patterson elaborates:

> Homemaking, if pursued with energy, imagination, and skills, has as much challenge and opportunity, success and failure, growth and expansion, perks and incentives as any corporation, plus something no other position offers—working for people you love most and want to please the most![7]

Through my mother's example and training, I caught a vision of the importance of my future mission. I knew that whether or not I got married, and no matter what other tasks God might have for me, I wanted to fulfill my biblical calling to be a "keeper of the home."

Today, although I may not be doing important works by society's standards, I am doing great things for God, by His grace. Although God did not call me to be a missionary in another country, I am able to share the gospel with my little boy, Jack. While I may not be an encouragement to thousands, I can pray for and encourage Steve, the godly man who is my husband. And I finally realized that I wasn't cut out to be a nurse, but each and every day I have the opportunity to serve the church and reach out to the community, all from the base of my home.

I know many other women, married and single, who are quietly and without fanfare starting a counterrevolution. They are intelligent, talented, godly visionaries who are seeking to change their world by answering God's call to be homemakers.

Carolyn McCulley is one such single woman. She has turned her back on the feminist ideology she formerly embraced and now enthusiastically serves others through her home. While she holds down a demanding job, she also thrives on hosting singles and married couples alike in her home for fellowship or evangelism (and even gourmet meals!). She loves to have children—especially her nieces and nephews—spend the night. In fact, Carolyn has recently written a book to encourage other single women to embrace God's feminine design.

Another revolutionary is my friend, Jonalee Earles, a young wife and mother. She was a straight-A student in high school who went on to study interior design and could have had her pick of career options. However, she's chosen to invest her creative talent into making a pleasant and delightful home for her husband and their three small children. Jonalee is a wonderful wife, an exceptional mom, and a skilled and artistic homemaker. In her spare time she helps other women decorate their homes.

Stephanie Pyle is a *future* homemaker. A bright college student at the local university, she does not hesitate to tell others that she hopes to make use of her degree as a wife and mother someday. Her fellow students are perplexed but curious. Stephanie is a young woman who has a clear vision of the importance of the home.

Carolyn, Jonalee, and Stephanie are participating in what one person called "the great task of renovating the world":

> Even if we cannot reform the world in a moment, we can begin the work by reforming ourselves and our households— It is woman's mission. Let her not look away from her own little family circle for the means of producing moral and social reforms, but begin at home.[8]

You want to join us? I must warn you that the world will not applaud you. Or worse, they may look down on you and criticize you. I guarantee there won't be awards given out for homemakers—at least, not in this world. And we probably won't see the effects right away. But our influence will surely outlast our lives.

Actually you don't have to wait until a future day or time to get started on your mission. You can begin today. We'll tell you how in the following chapter. But for the moment, consider: When the next person asks about your plans after high school, how will you respond? Will you join the vast number of women who have tossed away the keys to the home? Or will you join the homemaker's mission to change the world with the gospel?

For Further Study

❀ *Did I Kiss Marriage Goodbye?: Trusting God with a Hope Deferred* by Carolyn McCulley

❀ *Female Piety: A Young Woman's Friend and Guide* by John Angell James

❀ "The High Calling of Wife and Mother in Biblical Perspective" by Dorothy Patterson, in *Recovering Biblical Manhood & Womanhood*

Homemaking Internship

by Carolyn

Imagine preparing your whole life for a career in medicine. In high school you volunteer at the local hospital and spend your evenings reading medical journals. You make the honor roll and head off to a prestigious medical school. After eight years of only study and no social life, you finally graduate. Then you spend two, maybe three years in your chosen field—not even enough time to pay off the school loans.

But the more you practice medicine, the less you enjoy it. Suddenly you realize the truth. Your real calling is to be a teacher. You want to work with kids, small ones. So now with a mostly useless set of skills (at least you would know how to do the Heimlich maneuver if a kid choked on his hot dog in the school cafeteria), you want to enroll again at the university and study to be a teacher. But you can't. Your time and money have run out.

You can't afford to give six more years of your life to study, and you certainly can't afford the extra school debt. The years and the funds allotted for career preparation have already been spent on another profession. You have to accept the reality that you didn't graduate with the right degree to teach.

All too often we stumble onto homemaking the way this student stumbled onto teaching. We devote ourselves to studying for a particular career, but suddenly discover we want to enter an entirely different field for which we never prepared. Surprise! We find ourselves engaged to be married but without a degree in homemaking.

But unlike all other professions, we aren't forbidden from marrying simply because we aren't prepared. While teachers are not allowed to enter a classroom unless they have a diploma, every day women become wives, mothers, and homemakers with little or no preparation.

Girls often spend years of intensive study for other professions and yet are completely *un*prepared to assume the career of homemaking. As I wrote in my book *Feminine Appeal*, "Isn't it telling that our culture requires training and certification for so many vocations of lesser importance, but hands us marriage and motherhood without instruction?"[1] One author lamented:

> The fact is, our girls have no home education. When quite young they are sent to school where no feminine employment, no domestic habits, can be learned. . . . After this, few find any time to arrange, and make use of, the mass of elementary knowledge they have acquired; and fewer still have either leisure or taste for the inelegant, everyday duties of life. Thus prepared, they enter upon matrimony. Those early habits, which would have made domestic care a light and easy task, have never been taught, for fear it would interrupt their happiness; and the result is, that when cares come, as come they must, they find them misery. I am convinced that indifference and dislike between husband and wife are more frequently occasioned by this great error in education, than by any other cause.[2]

Although this author has accurately described the dismal state of education for the home today, she was actually writing in 1828. Only imagine what she would say were she alive to observe the situation now! If it's possible, girls are even *less* prepared now than they were 200 years ago. Young women tend to assume that homemaking doesn't require any advanced skills or preparation. It's similar to what a sixth grader might think about a test covering first-grade material: What's there to study?

But the truth is that homemaking involves so much more than just cleaning a house. The commands in Scripture to love, follow, and help a husband, to raise children for the glory of God, and to manage a home encompass a vast responsibility. Homemaking requires an extremely diverse array of skills—everything from management abilities, to knowledge of health and nutrition, to interior decorating capabilities, to childhood development expertise. If you are to become an effective homemaker, then you must study these subjects and many more.

And consider the potential number of years you may function as a wife, mother, and full-time homemaker. Obviously, this will differ for every woman, given the age we get married, bear children, and then the age we die. However, many of us will spend a considerable portion of our lives in the homemaking profession—from twenty or thirty to upwards of fifty years or more. That's no small amount of time in one career.

Most importantly, as we learned in the previous chapter, our homemaking mission is from *God*. For the majority of you who may be married someday, you will be called to support a husband and together to lead and train your children in godliness. And your home is to be a place from which the gospel goes forth.

So homemaking is a career that demands considerable expertise, may encompass decades of our lives, and has the potential to spread the gospel to our families, churches, communities, and future generations. Now that's a career worth preparing for, wouldn't you say?

Of course, it is not wrong to study for another career in addition to preparing for homemaking. However, the point is that we must not pursue any career to the neglect of training to be a homemaker. God has called us to be the keepers of the home; thus I want to urge you to give careful attention to your education for this profession.

You need not wait for home economics classes to once again

appear in high school and college syllabi. God did not assign this vital training to educational institutions. Instead, Scripture says that the older women should teach the young women to be effective home managers and to love their husbands and children (Titus 2:3-5). As with all other aspects of biblical womanhood, it is the mother's job to teach and the daughter's job to learn.

Mom, this is where you come in. I want to take a short intermission from our conversation with your daughter and speak with you for a moment. For the job of preparing our daughters to be homemakers—as we see from Titus 2:3-5—has been assigned to us as moms. And what an exciting task this is! We have the privilege of training our daughters to do what we love to do best—to be homemakers and world-changers for the gospel.

Mothers, we must begin by recognizing the full-time nature of our training. Remember Deuteronomy 6:7: "[You] shall talk of them when you sit in your house, and when you walk by the way, and when you lie down, and when you rise." We must incorporate domestic training into the fabric of our daily lives. We must seize every opportunity to prepare our daughters for their mission.

We should speak often to them about the joys of being a wife, mother, and homemaker. Because when you hang around someone who is enthusiastic about her career, it rubs off on you. So let's spread some homemaking enthusiasm to our daughters. But we must also advise them regarding the realities of homemaking. Many girls enter marriage and motherhood without a clue as to what's required, and they quickly fall into despair. We must tell our daughters of the sacrifices that homemaking demands—but also of the unsurpassed rewards it offers.

Besides the ongoing and impromptu teaching opportunities, we must set up a *structure* for training. A good domestic training plan must begin with the heart. As mothers, we must shape our daughters' convictions to reflect the biblical priority of the home. A steady diet of God's Word and other biblically informed materials are indispensable. (See "For Further Study," chapter 20.)

We must also continually orient our daughters' hearts to home life. This means—and I know this might be a radical concept—that our daughters need to *be* at home sometimes. I am aware from experience that this is not always easy during the teenage years, which are brimming over with options and activities. However, C. J. and I sought to preserve for our girls the priority of family and home. So family dinner each evening, weekly "Family Night," and other family-together events were nonnegotiable.

Finally, moms, an effective training program equips our daughters to manage all practical aspects of caring for a home and family. It is impossible to list here the numerous skills your daughter must possess. But if you simply reflect on your various daily responsibilities, it will provide a template from which you can develop a specific plan.

Think of your daughter as your homemaking intern. She needs both practical training and instruction. You can provide hands-on training by delegating portions of the household responsibilities to her for short periods of time. For example, you may assign your daughter to buy all the groceries and plan and cook all the meals for a week, or you may have her prepare dinner once a week on a consistent basis. Actually you could rotate through each section of your daily tasks in order to furnish your daughter with a well-rounded experience of the homemaker's world.

To provide your daughter with instruction in homemaking skills, you can get books from a library or bookstore on cleaning, organization, cooking, decorating, or childcare. You can also enroll together in one of the classes in the domestic arts offered by many county organizations or retail stores. My daughters and I have many fun memories from the courses we took on Chinese cooking, gift-wrapping, cake decorating, and more. If there is a homemaking skill in which you feel unequipped to instruct your daughter, contemplate asking a talented friend to teach her instead.

Practical training in homemaking skills should also be a factor in how you help your daughter approach her education. One man has observed:

> Women make academic decisions about course work and majors with little thought of the value of specific areas of knowledge for running a home, raising a family, or educating children. . . . Most . . . women, though, will be blessed by God with marriage and children and are therefore to raise up [their children] for the Lord. To fail to acknowledge this and make decisions accordingly in the critical years of life is so sad, really. Why should Christians join the world in despising housewifery and motherhood?[3]

Let's not despise homemaking and motherhood but rather honor it. Whether our daughters pursue a formal education or take a more unconventional learning track, let's make sure their season of learning includes preparation for their possible futures.

I encouraged my daughters to acquire skills that would not only benefit them in the workplace but would have lifelong returns as well. Nicole pursued writing opportunities, Kristin took college courses in accounting, and Janelle studied photography. They are all married today, and their respective abilities have enabled them to supplement their family incomes and serve others.

Finally, back to you, daughters. Let me encourage each of you to embrace your mother's domestic teaching. Allow her to probe your heart and direct your affections toward the home. And take it one step further. Appoint yourself as your mom's homemaking assistant. In addition to your assigned chores, be on the lookout for practical ways you can shoulder more of her homemaking responsibilities. In so doing, you will not only receive vital training for your future mission, but you will honor God by expressing your femininity today.

In conclusion, let me leave you with these words from John Angell James:

> My young friends, let it be your constant aim, and at the same time your earnest prayer, that you may first of all thoroughly understand your mission, and then diligently prepare for it, and hereafter as successfully fulfill it.[4]

22

A Girl's Reputation

by Carolyn

It is the ardent pursuit of many teenage girls. They want to be seen as cool. They want to be recognized as popular. This is the driving force behind the clothes they wear, the style of their hair, the way they talk, and whom they hang out with (or *wish* they could hang out with). However, Scripture tells us that we are to be known for something else. We are to be known for good works. Yes, you read that correctly. Good works.

Paul, in 1 Timothy 5:9-10, describes the godly woman as having "a reputation for good works" and living a life "devoted . . . to every good work." Although addressing the question about widows specifically, Paul is laying out God's standard for all of us in this passage. We are to cultivate a reputation for good works.

Have you seen the young lady who is devoted to good works lately? She may not be the most popular girl you know, but the more you hear about her, you find she's made a real difference in people's lives. She is always looking to serve. In fact, she's so busy thinking about others that she doesn't have a lot of time to think about herself. Although she doesn't do these good works to be noticed, she cannot escape our notice. Paul says that her good works are "conspicuous, and even those that are not cannot remain hidden" (1 Tim. 5:25).

So how about you—what is your reputation? Are you on a one-track quest for popularity, or are you known for your good works?

These good works are what Jerry Bridges calls "deliberate deeds that are helpful to others."[1] To speak the language of biblical womanhood, we must be dedicated to good works, beginning at home, and flowing outward into the church and community. The Bible says of the Proverbs 31 woman that she "looks well to the ways of her household" (v. 27). But it also says that she "opens her hand to the poor and reaches out her hands to the needy" (v. 20). From the base of her home, she launches out in good works for others. Following her example, the godly young woman should excel in good works.

In Matthew 5:16 we are told to "let your light shine before others, so that they may see your good works and *give glory to your Father who is in heaven*." Genuine good works don't point to us. They are like big neon signs that point to Christ. As John Stott writes, "It is when people see these [good works] . . . they will glorify God, for they embody the good news of his love which we proclaim."[2]

And what's really neat is that God has lined up good works for us to do. It says in Ephesians 2:10, "For we are his workmanship, created in Christ Jesus for good works, *which God prepared beforehand*, that we should walk in them" (emphasis added).

What does this mean? Well, recall with me for a moment craft time in kindergarten. Remember filing into the classroom, and on the table in front of each chair were little baggies filled with construction paper shapes? Glue and safety scissors and Popsicle sticks were all there too. The teacher had prepared the difficult part of the craft. All you had to do was glue it together, and before you knew it, you had a hand puppet or a Christmas ornament.

Good works are kind of like kindergarten crafts. God has them already laid out for us. We just need to do them. Which leads us to the question: What *are* the good works we are supposed to do? How will we recognize them when they come along? Does this mean that whenever we see someone in need, we're supposed to do something about it? No, and it's a good thing. There are so many opportunities for good works that if this were true, we would have to walk around with our eyes closed. But the good works that God has prepared for us are, most often, the opportunities closest to us. As Jerry Bridges points out, "God has created us to do our good works in the midst of the humdrum of daily living."[3]

Good works begin at home, right outside our bedroom door. When Paul addresses the children of widows in 1 Timothy 5:4, he tells them to "first learn to show godliness to their own household and to make some return to their parents, for this is pleasing in the sight of God." Doing good to our own family is a true evidence of our sincere love for Christ.

And may I suggest that there is probably no more worthy recipient of your good works than your mom. Observe her life for a single day, and you'll notice that she carries many responsibilities. She is constantly serving you and the other members of your family. So the best place to begin your good works quest may be by relieving her of a burden or two. You could start by cleaning your room. While you're at it, clean another room or two or cook a meal or do the dishes. Maybe you can even give your mom a backrub or surprise her with an encouraging note.

Charissa Galbraith, a young woman in our church, is noteworthy for her service to her mom, dad, and family. Charissa's younger brother Nathan was born with a medical condition that causes frequent and violent seizures. He requires constant care and attention. So night after night throughout her teenage years, Charissa took responsibility to care for Nathan. She would wake up, sometimes several times each night, to protect and comfort him during his seizures. Charissa's sacrifice of sleep allowed her mom to get much-needed rest so she could care for Nathan and their other six children during the day. Charissa is a young woman who is well-known for her good works to her family. Like Charissa, we should be devoted to good works for our families. And whether or not there are medical needs, there are doubtless many opportunities to bless your mom, as well as your dad, brothers, and sisters.

Serving in the home is only the beginning. The Bible also says that we are to "do good to everyone, and especially to those who are of the household of faith" (Gal. 6:10). As pastor Mark Dever has observed, "God doesn't call us to follow Christ alone. We're called to follow Christ together and with some particular people."[4] These "particular people" make up the local church in which God has placed us.

Deborah Banks has devoted herself to a variety of good works in our local church. All during high school, Deborah volunteered at the church office after school. In addition to that, this past summer she served an entire day each week. Deborah also gives of her time to help a young mom with many small children. And Deborah reaches out to new girls who come to church. She is a shining example of a young woman who has a reputation for good works.

The church where your family is involved is not just your parents' church. God has called *you* there as well. He has good works lined up for you to do in that particular church. In fact, God has given you unique gifts and talents specifically for use in your church. For example, Nora Jansen is a gifted caterer with artistic skill in flower arranging. She puts her God-given gifts to use by serving many brides who get married in our church, and she decorates for church functions.

Maybe you have musical ability, or perhaps you are good with children or talented in drama. You might have a knack for organizing events, or you may simply be a faithful servant. No doubt there are countless ways you can devote yourself to good works in your church. Consider asking your mom, dad, and pastor how you can serve.

Finally, the godly young woman is to reach out and do good to *all* people. After we have served the believers in our local church, we must extend our good works to the community around us.

Jessica Loftness is one young woman with an eye for reaching out. At her brother's baseball game, Jessica met a girl named Laura and befriended her. Soon Laura began coming to church with Jessica and even attended an evangelistic program at our church where she put her trust in Christ. However, it didn't end there. Laura began inviting more people to church—her mom and other friends. Jessica's faithfulness to do good to Laura resulted in her salvation and in turn affected others. Way to go, Jessica!

Charissa, Deborah, Nora, and Jessica are sterling examples of devotion to good works. By following their lead, you will give evidence of your genuine faith and bring much glory to God. I realize, however, that good works can be exhausting at times. And yet the Lord reminds us in Galatians 6:8-10:

> *The one who sows to his own flesh will from the flesh reap corruption, but the one who sows to the Spirit will from the Spirit reap eternal life. And let us not grow weary of doing good, for in due season we will reap, if we do not give up. So then, as we have opportunity, let us do good to everyone.*

May this promise energize you to press on and devote yourself to good works!

We hope by now that you are starting to recognize the portrait of the godly young woman. She enjoys her God-given feminine design. She is a young woman of true beauty and modesty who fears her God and is a faithful friend. She is committed to absolute purity in her relationships with guys. And she is eager to fulfill her homemaking mission and do good works for others. Now it is time to turn the page and observe how the godly young woman walks through courtship and into marriage.

For Further Study

❀ *Stop Dating the Church: Fall in Love with the Family of God* by Joshua Harris

When It Comes to Courtship

by Carolyn

Little did I know that on the night Brian Chesemore came to dinner, it signaled the beginning of a whole new adventure in my daughter's life—the adventure of courtship. When Brian asked C. J. for permission to court Kristin, and permission was given, it meant that, ready or not, it was time to guide her through this wonderful and yet unpredictable season.

During the next five years, I walked with each of my three daughters through a courtship process. No two were alike. Their respective courtships were as uniquely different as my daughters themselves. But the emotions I experienced as a mother were the same each time. There was the joy and excitement of watching my daughter fall in love and observing God's handiwork in bringing two people together. But the anxious questions weren't far behind: "What if this doesn't work out? What if she changes her mind? What if he backs out, and she gets hurt? Are they really right for each other? How do we help our daughter discern God's will? Have I fully prepared her for this? How will she know if he's the one?"

What quieted my many worries was the truth that God's Word contains all the wisdom and guidance we mothers need to help our daughters navigate the sometimes tricky waters of courtship. After giving us clear direction for the training of the godly young woman, God does not leave us in the dark when it comes time to help our daughters consider a potential spouse.

Now this chapter is by no means a thorough study of God's Word on the subject of courtship. I will merely attempt to offer a few points of biblical guidance to assist mothers in counseling their daughters through this process. However, I want to highly recommend author and friend Joshua Harris's two books on relationships: *I Kissed Dating Goodbye* and *Boy Meets Girl*. Together they provide a comprehensive and invaluable guide to God's Word as applied to courtship, love, and romance.

I want to add that ideally a young girl's father bears the primary responsibility to lead his daughter in decisions regarding courtship and marriage. However, your role as a mother is critical. You play a key part in assisting your husband to lead by bringing your insight and wisdom to the process. As your daughter's friend, you also have a special opportunity to share in her joys, empathize with her struggles, and offer biblical counsel for her many questions.

As parents, we must begin by helping our daughters cultivate a trust in God for what appears to be an uncertain future. We must emphasize the importance of trusting God for whom they will marry, when they will marry, and even *if* they will marry. We must teach them to place their hopes for the future in the kindness and faithfulness of God. "For I know the plans I have for you," He declares in Jeremiah 29:11, "plans . . . to give you a future and a hope." Those who trust in the Lord will never ultimately be disappointed. They will be able to face an uncertain future with confident joy.

Most young women, however, will enter into a courtship relationship someday. When that day arrives for your daughter, you must help her put romantic feelings in their proper place. Let me say up front that romantic feelings are a necessary aspect of any relationship headed for marriage. However, they must not be your daughter's main guide in her decision to accept or reject a young man's proposal. For example, I have known young women to make disastrous choices simply because they had a "strong feeling" that a particular young man was "the one." I have also observed young women who were uncertain and indecisive regarding marriage because they put too much stock in how they felt from day to day.

All feelings—including romantic feelings—find their origin in thoughts and beliefs. If your daughter has strong feelings for an ungodly young man, you must help her pinpoint the sin that gives rise to such feelings. Similarly, vacillating emotions related to the prospect of marriage may indicate the presence of fear and the absence of faith, or worldly criteria for evaluating a potential husband. When feelings take their proper place as a necessary part but not the final authority in the process, a young woman can walk through courtship with peace and joyful expectation of God's goodness.

A biblical view of romantic feelings must be coupled with sound biblical criteria for evaluating a young man as a potential spouse. When my own daughters faced that enormous question—"Is he the one?"—C. J. and I sought to help them measure that young man by God's standard. This provided our daughters with clarity and comfort as they sorted through crazy emotions on their way to making that life-altering decision.

Often young women create a detailed profile of the man they want to marry. They spend their youth and single years refining their "list": what he will look like or *not* look like, what kind of personality he will have, and what his interests and hobbies will be. While some of their criteria may be good and even godly, this can be an unwise and unhelpful practice.

We must not allow our daughters to presume that they can dictate to God their requirements for a husband. This isn't a Christmas list, and God is not a cosmic Santa Claus. Rather we must help them stick to a standard of character from the Bible and leave the guy's hair color and personality up to God. As

Elisabeth Elliot advises young people from experience, "The will of God is always *different* from what they expect; always *bigger,* and ultimately, infinitely more *glorious* than their wildest imaginings."[1]

C. J. and I sought to provide our daughters with a "list" from Scripture. While not exhaustive, the following characteristics comprised the essentials for any man desirous of pursuing our daughters:

1. *Genuine passion for God.* The greatest commandment is to "love the Lord your God with all your heart and with all your soul and with all your mind" (Matt. 22:37). A mere profession of faith is insufficient. A godly man will consistently display love, obedience, and increasing passion for the Savior.

2. *Authentic humility.* "This is the one to whom I will look," says the Lord, "he who is humble and contrite in spirit and trembles at my word" (Isa. 66:2). Your daughter will marry a sinner— that is certain. But if he is a humble and teachable sinner who is quick to repent, then he will be sure to grow in godliness. This humility will also be evident in his love for and submission to God's Word.

3. *Love for the local church.* At the center of God's plan on earth is His church. A young man must be pursuing fellowship and serving faithfully in a local church if he is to make a good candidate for a husband.

4. *Biblical convictions about manhood and womanhood.* A successful marriage is due in large part to the couple's grasp of their respective roles and responsibilities. A potential husband must be committed to the complementary roles found in Scripture. He must be ready to embrace his responsibility to love and lead his wife (Eph. 5:22-25).

In addition to comparing the young man to this list of essentials, we also helped our daughters evaluate God's commands to wives. From Scripture we asked our daughters the following questions regarding the young man each was considering:

❀ Do you fully respect this man the way a wife is called to respect her husband?

❀ Can you eagerly submit to him as the church submits to Christ?

❀ Do you have faith to follow this man no matter where he may lead?

❀ Can you love this man with a tender, affectionate love? (1 Cor. 11:3; Eph. 5:22, 33; Col. 3:18; Titus 2:4-5)

These criteria and questions can protect your daughter from pursuing a relationship with or even marrying an unworthy young man. They can also boost her faith and confidence for marriage to a godly young man—as they did for my daughters.

Daughters, obviously this topic of love and marriage is of great significance. That's why God has supplied His Word. It's also why He has given you parents to guide you through this often exciting and sometimes confusing process. Please don't minimize or ignore their counsel. Bring your parents, and especially your mom, into the details of your thoughts and questions on this subject. Open up to them the inner workings of your heart long before a decision arrives on your doorstep. Their counsel and guidance will protect you from foolish choices and result in blessings for the rest of your life.

Each courtship, whether or not it ends in marriage, is its own unique journey. But God has provided all the wisdom that we need in His Word. So let us mothers and daughters (and fathers too!) trust Him and seek His good and perfect will.

For Further Study

❀ *I Kissed Dating Goodbye* by Joshua Harris
❀ *Boy Meets Girl: Say Hello to Courtship* by Joshua Harris

24

Who Gives This Woman?

by Carolyn

It was a crazy idea, but it was what you would expect from Janelle. As a small girl, my youngest daughter sported an impish grin and gleaming blue eyes. Wherever she went, mischief and fun trailed behind, as close as her well-worn "blankey." If she was quiet for more than five minutes, it was time to send the scouts—her sisters—to discover what mess she'd created this time.

Her memorable antics included smearing her entire room with Vaseline petroleum jelly, "losing" her shoes at the shoe store so we would have to buy her a new pair, and wandering off in the department store and taking the escalator to the candy counter where we found her happily munching on Godiva chocolate. Over time our family grew fond of inserting her name in that well-known song from the *Sound of Music*: "How do you solve a problem like *Janelley*?"

Now my playful girl was all grown up and getting married, and in typical Janelle style, she wanted to have a *surprise* wedding. So we spread the word of her engagement, but in the following weeks and months we planned the entire wedding—*in secret*. We made clandestine visits to the bridal shop with her sisters and their babies in tow. We held undercover meetings with a wedding team in charge of setup, food, and decorations. We sent classified e-mails to the bridal party and scheduled the dress rehearsal for 10 P. M. when the church building would be deserted.

Why all this trouble, you might ask? She thought it would be fun to invite the entire church, adults and children alike, to her wedding. She even planned the reception with the kids in mind, complete with moon bounces and ice cream sundaes. Janelle desired to make a memory that would bless our church—the dearest people to our family's hearts.

On the first Sunday in June, Janelle fidgeted in her seat at church, trying not to let on that today was one of the happiest days of her life. My husband, C. J., the senior pastor of our church, approached the podium to make the formal announcement everyone had been expecting: "It is my privilege and joy this morning to announce the engagement of Michael Bradshaw to Janelle Mahaney."

After the clapping and cheering subsided, he continued, "And we would like to invite all of you to the wedding on June 1, 2003, at 3:00 P. M." A confused silence, followed by laughter, rippled across the room as people mentally realized the date—June 1, 2003. Today! Then at once the entire congregation began to cheer and applaud their approval. And that all-too-familiar playful smile spread across Janelle's face. *It worked!*

For the third and final time I stood as matron of honor at one of my daughters' weddings. The steadfast faithfulness of God caused me to marvel once again. For I knew it was not extraordinary mothering that had produced these young women. It was extraordinary grace, poured out in spite of my weaknesses and shortcomings.

I remembered with a smile how often I had lifted exasperated hands to heaven, crying out to God for the wisdom to mother these three girls. And I thanked Him on that wedding day for answering my prayers.

"Who gives this woman to this man?" The question broke my reverie.

"Her mother and I . . ."

Today my husband and I were presenting our third daughter to a godly young man in marriage. As happy as I was to see God's good plan for Janelle unfold, the finality of the exchange left me saddened. This wasn't the first time I had felt this way.

While Kristin and Nicole didn't have surprise weddings (in fact, each wedding was dramatically different, just like my girls), one thing was the same: In the twenty minutes from "Who gives this woman?" to "I do," our relationship was irrevocably altered. I was *giving* them to another. It was harder than I had expected.

The joys and challenges of leading each of my daughters on the bumpy and exciting road to biblical womanhood had forged a tight bond between us—just *how* tight I discovered only when I faced the imminent prospect of turning them over to another.

My first warning bell had sounded the night that Brian asked permission to court Kristin. A year later they were married, and they moved—too far away—to Chicago to help plant a church. It's a good thing Brian is such a godly young man and was headed out to serve the Lord. Otherwise, I'm not sure I would have let him take my daughter away. Just kidding. But needless to say, I was delighted when they returned two years ago so Brian could come on staff at our church, Covenant Life Church.

Nicole's knight in shining armor surprised all of us two years later by riding up in a red Jeep Wrangler (Nicole's not exactly a Jeep kind of girl). He proposed with lines from Shakespeare that became the theme of their wedding. They settled a bit closer, just across the river in northern Virginia where Steve now serves as a youth pastor. Fortunately, Mike and Janelle stayed nearby and also serve with us at Covenant Life.

Each of my daughters' engagements marked the commencement of a transition, one that became official on their wedding day. The time before a daughter's wedding is a gift of mercy to a mother. It's our chance to put the finishing touches on our handiwork, to give our daughter the concluding instructions before she becomes a wife and mother.

It is absolutely vital that we facilitate the transfer of all our daughter's affections, trust, submission, and service to her husband. We must teach her to look to her husband in all decisions, to seek his spiritual guidance, to submit to his leadership, to follow him wholeheartedly wherever he may go, and to pour all her effort into making him a success.

My daughters and I each had many conversations in the days leading up to their weddings—and not just about bridesmaid dresses and invitations. For years I had sought to teach them about the realities and joys of marriage and motherhood. But the lessons had more urgency and more specificity now. We talked about lovemaking, about conflict, and about the unique challenges they might face. I tried to seize every opportunity to make them as ready as possible.

But then on their wedding day, I had to relinquish all rights, expectations, and desires. Unequivocally. No exceptions. I'm not saying this was easy. It was the hardest duty I ever had to perform as a mother—to turn over my life's work to someone else. But as mothers, we must not allow these naturally strong emotions to justify selfish behavior. We must release our daughters completely.

What compelled and sustained me through this bittersweet season was the fear of the Lord. He has created marriage to reflect His glory, and I did not want to dishonor Him by seeking to undermine His good and perfect will. I was reminded in Ephesians that "a man shall leave his father and mother and hold fast to his wife, and the two shall become one flesh" (Eph. 5:31). "Leave and cleave," we say as shorthand, using the older King James language.

We must remember, dear mothers, that these daughters were never really ours, but the Lord's. By releasing them to their husbands, we are simply reaffirming what has always been true. Elisabeth Elliot says that her godly parents were sobered by this truth:

> It was not easy for our parents to let us go. They knew from the start that they were trustees, not owners, of the children

God had given them. We were not their property. We had been lent to them for a time, a sacred trust of which they were the divinely assigned trustees. A time came when that trust had been discharged.[1]

Our daughters, it says in Psalm 127:4, are "like arrows in the hand of a warrior." Arrows are not crafted merely to look attractive in the quiver. They are designed to fly to meet their mark. So it is with our daughters. We must send them out to accomplish the mission of biblical womanhood, to bring glory to the gospel. We are only successful in passing on our language of biblical womanhood if we complete this task.

However, my relationship with my daughters did not end the day they got married. It simply changed. While their husbands are now their best friends (and I wouldn't have it any other way), we now share the new and sweet fellowship of married women. In many ways, we are closer today than ever before. And their husbands are now their leaders and the objects of their affection; however, I am still called to fulfill the biblical role of what Titus 2 calls the older woman in their lives.

Our mothering efforts to preserve the language of biblical womanhood do not end at the marriage altar, but they take a completely different form. As mothers, we don't just sit down, shut up, and hope our daughters will remember what we've told them. More than ever, as married women, they need our help to successfully love and care for their husbands, children, and homes.

I fulfill this role primarily by directing my daughters to their husbands. If one of my daughters calls me with a spiritual question or a problem, I ask, "What does your husband say?" My goal is to constantly reinforce and support his God-appointed leadership in her life. It didn't take long for my sons-in-law to realize that I was one of their greatest allies. Soon they were encouraging their wives to "ask your mom what she thinks."

Another way I try to serve my daughters is through my encouragement, correction, and counsel in all matters related to biblical womanhood. I exhort them to grow in respect and love for their husbands. I encourage them to persevere through the challenges of motherhood. I seek to spur them on to bring glory to the gospel in all aspects of their homemaking responsibilities. I am also on call to answer the myriad of practical questions that inevitably fluster the new wife and mom. "How do I cook a twenty-pound turkey?" and "What laundry detergent do I use for baby clothes?" and "Does this picture match the color of my living room?" Now I have the immense joy of baby-sitting my grandsons and giving my daughters the occasional day off to read and seek the Lord or catch up on sleep.

Moms, let's position ourselves to serve our daughters, their husbands, and our grandchildren, practically and spiritually. Now is not the time to move on to our own selfish pursuits, but to humbly and strategically invest our gifts, energies, and time into helping our daughters fulfill *their* mission—to live out and to pass on the language of biblical womanhood to the *next* generation of young women.

Oh, and I must confess that I did make one small request of my sons-in-law before I agreed to relinquish my daughters. I asked to have the girls back for one twenty-four-hour period each year. I asked for the Shopping Trip. And each one graciously agreed. Thank you, Steve, Brian, and Mike. I am in your debt—and not just for the Shopping Trip, but for the exceptional way that each of you love and lead my daughters.

25

Passing on the Language of Biblical Womanhood

Carolyn & Nicole

Now it is time for the end of the story. We began our journey together by telling you the history of the Nushu language: the girls-only writing script created and preserved by Chinese women for over fifteen hundred years. Today the Nushu language is dying. There may be only a handful of women alive who can read and write the delicate characters. In twenty years, Nushu may cease to be used altogether. That's because the girls in China now learn to read and write Chinese along with the boys. Nushu, for these girls, holds little appeal.[1]

Likewise the continued existence of our own unique language of biblical womanhood is threatened. Our society scorns the virtues of modesty, purity, and love for the home. And, sad to say, many in the church have been seduced and have conformed to the culture as well.

However, not only are these virtues scorned; our language is under fierce attack. Countless people have dedicated their lives to eradicate the language of biblical womanhood from the earth. You'll find them in the fashion industry, in Hollywood, on television, in the media, in music, and in education. They are publishers of magazines and authors of books and even presidents of political organizations.

They want to silence the language of biblical womanhood forever. Their attacks are both brazen and subtle. While openly mocking our God-given language, they dress up their ungodly language as harmless, fun, and satisfying.

"Experts" tear down the mother-daughter relationship by implying that Mom is irrelevant and out of touch. They put forth peers and other counselors as more reliable sources of guidance and friendship.

Television, movies, and music promote promiscuity and immorality with tantalizing images and words. Condoms are freely distributed to young people. The message: Sex before marriage is normal; purity is impossible.

Magazines laud idleness, gossip, and vanity. "Learn a juicy secret;" "Indulge yourself;" "Follow your dreams," they prattle. Selflessness and good works get in the way of their agenda.

Authors blur and confuse the differences between men and women. They insist that a girl can do whatever a guy does and that our biological differences are irrelevant. Thus, femininity is emptied of its purpose and meaning.

The educational system prepares a young woman for every career except homemaking. Full-time wives and mothers are looked down upon as lazy underachievers. Honor and recognition are reserved for those who leave family responsibilities behind.

The beautiful model with her makeup, clothing, and jewelry proclaims that physical beauty is supreme. There is no praise for the gentle and quiet spirit.

Retail stores lay out a plethora of tight and skimpy clothing. The way to get attention, they promise, is to show off more skin. Modesty is portrayed as unattractive and pointless.

In all they say and do, there is no fear of God before their eyes.

The result is that for many young girls today, the language of biblical womanhood holds little appeal. The future of *girl talk* hangs in the balance.

So now, more than ever before, we must be faithful to pass on the language of biblical womanhood from mother to daughter. We must not stand by and see this treasured language stamped out by the opponents of God's Word. We must devote all our energies to faithfully and unashamedly exhibit these qualities in the context of everyday life, in full view of the world around us.

That is why it is vital to forge strong mother-daughter relationships. Together we must prove that purity is possible and that homemaking is honorable. We must parade a beauty that does not rely on outward adornment. We must put good works on full display.

In so doing, we will silence the opponents of the gospel. Mothers and daughters, whose conduct is consistent with the message they profess, put the critics to shame. Scripture says they will have "nothing evil to say about us" (Titus 2:8). We give them no opportunity to dismiss or ignore the gospel. By speaking the language of biblical womanhood, we disarm the enemies of God's Word.

And what's more, the language of biblical womanhood presents the gospel as attractive (Titus 2:10). It says to our hostile culture, "Come and see the beauty of the gospel." When the world catches a glimpse of a mother and daughter enjoying their friendship or gazes at a girl who dresses modestly and does not strive for attention, when they observe a young woman ambitious to serve in the home and do good works in the church, when they detect the heart of a true friend or the loveliness of purity, these qualities will provoke their curiosity.

And that is why, as mothers and daughters, we must speak the language of biblical womanhood: for the sake of the gospel. Our unique language declares with a happy shout, "the grace of God has appeared, bringing salvation for all people" (Titus 2:11). It joyfully tells how "our great God and Savior Jesus Christ . . . gave himself for us to redeem us" (Titus 2:13-14).

But this language must not simply end with us—mother and

daughter. Psalm 78:4 is our solemn charge: "We will not hide them from their children, but *tell to the coming generation the glorious deeds of the LORD*, and his might, and the wonders that he has done." The words of songwriter Sara Groves echo our heart cry: "Remind me of this with every decision, generations will reap what I sow. I can pass on a curse or a blessing to those I will never know. To my great-great-great-granddaughter, live in peace."[2]

Someday a little girl will be born in a time and age we will never see. Will she hear the saving message of the gospel? Will her mother whisper the sweet language of biblical womanhood softly in her ear? Will she adorn the truth in the ungodly culture in which *she* lives?

Oh, that God would give us grace to pass on our mother-daughter language of biblical womanhood so that our great-great-great-granddaughters will receive and reflect the glorious message of the gospel!

For Further Study

❀ *Evangelical Feminism and Biblical Truth* by Wayne Grudem
❀ *The Legacy of Biblical Womanhood* by Susan Hunt and Barbara Thompson

Appendix A
GIRL TALK
Discussion Questions

So, Mom, you're ready for *girl talk,* but you need a little help to get the conversation started? Well, you've come to the right place. We've created questions just for you and your daughter, based on the content of this book. We hope they spark many gospel-centered talks about the language of biblical womanhood. Also included are application suggestions or optional activities to help you grow in your relationship.

These questions (in italics) are meant for you to ask your daughter. (Instructions are in regular type.) However, by first answering the questions yourself, you will make it easier for your daughter to share. We recommend scheduling a series of times to go through these questions together. And when you've run out of chapters, you will find more questions to ask each other in Appendix B that will help keep communication flowing. Happy talking!

PART ONE

Chapter One

1. *Between a one and a ten, what was your excitement level when I told you we were going through this book together? (One = I would rather go to the dentist and get a root canal; Ten = I've already finished the book!)*

2. Read Titus 2:3-14. *What is God's purpose for our mother-daughter relationship, and why is it important?*

3. *What is the definition of biblical womanhood?* From Proverbs

31:10-31, 1 Timothy 5:9-10, Titus 2:3-5, and 1 Peter 3:1-6 work together to create a list of the qualities of biblical womanhood.

4. Have your daughter pick one quality from the list you compiled. *What does it look like for you to demonstrate this quality in everyday life? How can I more effectively demonstrate this same quality? What is the result when we display the qualities of biblical womanhood?*

5. *What is one quality from our list that is unpopular or ignored by your peers? Why do you think this is true?*

6. *Strong mother-daughter relationships are vital to the preservation of our language of biblical womanhood. Would you describe our relationship as strong? Why or why not?*

7. *What is one way you hope our relationship will grow stronger and closer as a result of reading, discussing, and applying what's in this book?* Write your daughter's answer down for review at the conclusion of reading *Girl Talk.*

End with prayer, thanking God for your daughter and asking Him to help you forge a strong mother-daughter relationship through which you can successfully pass on the language of biblical womanhood that commends the gospel.

Mother: Optional Activity

Present your daughter with an heirloom from her grandmother, a relative, or from you. Explain why this is a gift you hope she will treasure. Also tell her about the most important legacy you hope she will receive from you—a legacy of biblical womanhood.

Chapter Two

1. *What are some funny ways that you and I are different from each other (looks, personality, interests, etc.)? How are we alike?*

2. *What do Psalm 139:16 and Acts 17:26 (NIV) tell us about the origins of our mother-daughter relationship?*

3. *How does the fact that God has put us together as mother and daughter help you think about our relationship—and even about our differences?*

4. *Do you think I've allowed any of our differences or disagreements to get in the way of our relationship? Have you? Tell me more about your answers.*

5. *In what specific ways are you and I the perfect combination for passing on the language of biblical womanhood?*

Mother and Daughter: Special Assignment

Write a note to each other, describing one character trait you appreciate in the other person and telling how this quality is helping you grow in biblical womanhood.

Chapter Three

1. *Nicole couldn't find Mom in a popular teen magazine. What are other places where moms are missing from the messages of our culture?*

2. *Among your peers who are the popular mom-replacements— the confidantes, friends, and counselors they look to instead of to their moms?*

3. Take time together to look up the Scriptures from Proverbs referenced in this chapter. *What does God say in the Bible about the importance of my role in your life? What blessings will result from my influence?*

4. *If your life were a magazine where would I appear? Why?*

5. *How do you feel about my involvement in your life? What are the reasons for your answer? How does your answer compare to what the Bible says?*

6. Review the questions on page 39 with your daughter. *Do you think I am the primary influence in your life? Why or why not? How can I make it easier for you to confide in me?*

Daughter: Application

Share with your mom one situation you are struggling with or confused about and ask for her advice. Look out for the blessings that will come from your mom's influence!

Chapter Four

1. *What is your favorite activity that we do as mother and daughter? Do we spend enough time just having fun? What fun ideas do you have of things we can do together?* (For more ideas, see Appendix D.)

2. *According to this chapter, why is it important for me to be actively involved in your life, especially during your teenage years?*

3. *Give an example of a difficult situation you have faced in the past or are facing now. How did or how can my involvement as your mother make a difference?*

4. *Do you think that you are more enthusiastic or less enthusiastic about spending time with me than when you were a young girl? Why?*

5. *Do you think that you have constructed a moat around yourself or resisted my involvement in your life? If so, why?* Humbly share your perspective about your daughter's heart toward you.

6. *Could you relate to any of the reasons that Nicole and Kristin pushed their mom away and didn't want to go on Afternoon Out?*

7. *Do you think our relationship is one of my highest priorities? Why or why not?*

Mother and Daughter: Optional Activity

Plan your own Afternoon Out and spend time just having fun!

Chapter Five

1. *What is the funniest conversation you and I have ever had? Who gets the award for "best talker"—me or you?*

2. Read Deuteronomy 6:4-9. *How many of the five girl talk principles for mother-daughter communication can you repeat without looking?*

3. *How would you rate our communication between a one and a ten? (One— "Pass the butter"; Ten— "God has been teaching me . . .") How can I make it better?*

4. *The first girl talk principle is:* Godly mother-daughter communication starts with Mom. *How well do I do at initiating conversation with you? How well do you think that you respond?*

5. *What is your biggest obstacle to freely sharing your heart with me?*

6. *What's your favorite time for mother-daughter talks?*

7. *Do I set an example of open and honest communication with you? How can I improve? Now let me ask you: Is there anything that you need to tell me?*

8. *How does the fifth girl talk principle give us hope for better communication?* Godly mother-daughter communication is possible through the grace of God.

Mother: Application

Schedule a regular communication time for you and your daughter.

Chapter Six

1. Reminisce about an argument that you and your daughter can laugh at now.

2. *What are the three things that we must remember in order to find our way out of Conflict Jungle?*

3. *Which of the phrases on page 59 (or similar phrases) have you used to describe our differences? Have you ever heard me use one of these phrases? What words does God use to explain our conflict?*

4. *What does Scripture say is the source of all of our quarrels and fights (see James 4:1-2)?*

5. Choose one common conflict between you and your daughter (e.g., not cleaning up her room). Confess what you have been craving (wanting) in that situation and ask for her forgiveness. Then ask your daughter: *What do you think that you have been sinfully craving in this conflict?*

6. *On page 61, Nicole shares Paul Tripp's rule: "Deal with yourself before you deal with your teenager." Do I follow this advice?*

7. *How does 1 John 1:9 and the message of the gospel give us hope to resolve our conflicts?*

Mother and Daughter: Application

The next time you are in a conflict, stop and read this chapter again before continuing your discussion. Then talk about why your conflict is *worse than you think, simpler than you think,* and *easier to resolve than you think.* Repent and ask each other's forgiveness if necessary.

Chapter Seven

Mother: Application

If you are consistently tempted to forecast defeat instead of victory, read *Trusting God* by Jerry Bridges.

Chapter Eight

1. *Do you observe any habit in my life where I do not practice what I preach? If so, please describe it.*

2. *If there is one thing about me you could change, what would it be?*

3. *How has my example inspired you to trust and follow God?*

Mother: Application

If you are convicted of inconsistency between your example and your instruction, humble yourself and ask God and then your daughter for forgiveness. Your humility will be a wonderful example for your daughter to follow.

Chapter Nine

1. *Are you confident of my love for you? If not, what would cause you to doubt my love?*

2. *In what ways do you most commonly experience my love and affection?*

3. *Do you think that I remember what it was like to "live in*

the scary world of the teen years"? How can I better empathize with you?

Mother: Application

Choose one of the ideas from this chapter for expressing tender love and find a way to put it into practice this week.

Chapter Ten

1. *Which phrase best describes your passion for the Lord: "on fire," "lukewarm," or "cold"? Tell me more about your answer.*

2. *Do you have any questions about a decision that I (and your dad) have made for you? Are there any decisions with which you disagree? Why?* Spend as much time as necessary to answer your daughter's questions and discuss her disagreements.

3. *Are you convinced that our discipline springs from a tender love? Why or why not?*

4. *Has there been a past decision you didn't understand or agree with that you are grateful for now? Elaborate.*

Mother: Application

If your daughter's heart is lukewarm or if there is an area of sin you need to address, then along with your husband discuss and develop a plan of action to help her grow in godliness.

Chapter Eleven

1. *What is the scariest movie you have ever seen?*

2. *According to the Bible, why is disrespect toward Mom (and Dad) so serious?*

3. *In what ways are you tempted to dishonor me in your heart, words, or actions?* Encourage your daughter not to be afraid to answer honestly.

4. *What excuses are you sometimes tempted to make for not showing me honor? What does the Bible say about the validity of these excuses?*

5. *What hope is there for the daughter who dishonors her mother?*

Daughter: Application

Using the list on page 89-90?, choose one way to show honor to your mom this week.

Chapter Twelve

1. *Have I ever told you to do something that was the last thing in the world you wanted to do? What was it?*
2. *Describe true obedience. Do you think that you obey me in attitude as well as in action? Explain your answer.*
3. *Would you consider yourself "hungry" for wisdom? Do you have faith for my God-given authority in your life? Why or why not?*
4. *Why did God establish parental authority? What blessings does God promise when we obey?*
5. *Why is disobedience a dangerous choice? How does God's mercy cover our disobedience?*

Daughter: Application

If you have not obeyed your mother with your whole heart, then confess your disobedience to the Lord and to your mom. Pray along with your mom that God would change your heart. Don't wait to feel different. Begin to obey.

PART TWO
Chapter Thirteen

1. *Has our relationship grown closer since we started reading this book? If so, in what ways?*
2. *When is the best time to begin learning the language of biblical womanhood? Why?*
3. *What is so exciting about the language of biblical womanhood? What do you think about that?*

Chapter Fourteen

1. *How should the fact that God created us affect the way we think about our femininity?*

2. *Genesis 2:18 introduces us to our unique feminine purpose. What is it?*

3. *What is one way you can express your feminine design and assist someone by being supportive?*

4. *How well do you cooperate with and respond to the authority God has placed over you? In other words, how well do you think you express the feminine quality of responsiveness? Explain your answer.*

5. *Think of one way you have shown "an inclination to provide support and care for others." How did it make you feel to nurture and care for someone else?*

6. *Do you have an area where you find it difficult to express your feminine design? Why? How can I help?*

7. *Before reading this chapter, would you have thought of expressing your femininity the way God intended as "fun"? What do you think now?*

Mother and Daughter: Optional Service Project

Consider visiting residents at a local nursing home, giving a mom with young children a day out, or pooling your resources and sponsoring a needy child.

Chapter Fifteen

1. *When was the last time you faced a decision to fear the Lord or follow the crowd? What did you do and why?*

2. *How closely does your profile match that of the godly girl who fears the Lord? Encourage your daughter for the ways you observe the fear of the Lord in her life.*

3. *Is there any situation where you are currently ensnared by the fear of man? How can the fear of God protect you from the fear of man?*

4. *How can you recognize the girl who chooses to fear the Lord?*

5. *How can I help you to overcome the fear of man and become a woman who fears the Lord?*

Mother and Daughter: Application

Spend some time praying together that God would help both of you to grow in the fear of the Lord.

Chapter Sixteen

1. *Who would you consider to be your best friends? Why are they your friends?*

2. *According to the Bible, do we need friends? Give a Scripture to back up your answer.*

3. *What are some of the qualities of a biblical friend? Do your friends possess these qualities? Are you this kind of friend?*

4. *Do you think I possess the qualities of a biblical friend?* Talk about your mother-daughter friendship.

5. *What are some of the characteristics of an ungodly friend? Does this describe any of your friends?*

6. *Why is Jesus the best of friends?*

Daughter: Application

Ask your mom to help you do a "friendship inventory." Make a list of all your friends or potential friends. Consider which friendships (if any) are an ungodly influence and may need to change. Who are the godly friends you can pursue instead?

Chapter Seventeen

1. *What is God's standard of purity? What are the three weapons that we must employ in our fight for purity?*

2. *In what areas are you tempted to "make provision for the flesh"? How can you avoid these situations in the future?*

3. How comfortable do you feel talking with me about guys? Elaborate on your answer.

4. How can I help you in your quest for purity?

5. What do you think about the guidelines for sharing about crushes that Nicole's mom set in place?

6. How closely does your own standard of purity resemble God's standard? Is there any sin of impurity that you need to confess to me?

Daughter: Application

If she doesn't already know, tell your mom today whom you have a crush on.

Chapter Eighteen

1. Do you have a physical feature you're not fond of? What is it? What is that feature's kingdom purpose? Tell your daughter why you think she is beautiful.

2. Why are girls and women so obsessed with beauty? Are you obsessed with physical beauty? Explain your answer. What does the Bible say that physical beauty achieves (Prov. 31:30)?

3. What does 1 Peter 3:3 mean by saying, "Do not let your adorning be external"? What beauty does God require?

4. How can you display a gentle and quiet spirit? What will be the result?

Mother and Daughter: Optional Activity

Go get a facial or a manicure together. Then go for coffee and discuss the beauty questions on pages 134-135.

Chapter Nineteen

1. What did you think about Jack's and Jason's comments about modest women?

2. What was your opinion of modesty before reading this chapter? Has it changed, and, if so, how?

3. Why is modesty so important? How can you protect guys through your dress?

Mother and Daughter: Application

Time for some wardrobe examinations. Answer the questions in the "Modesty Heart Check," Appendix E. Go through your closet first and then your daughter's.

Chapter Twenty

1. When people ask what you are going to do after high school, what do you say?

2. What is a woman's mission, and why is it so significant?

3. In what ways have you observed our culture undermine the importance of God's calling to women to be "keepers of the home"?

4. Describe your opinions of "homemaking" as a career. Has your thinking about your future changed since reading this chapter? If so, how?

5. Have you been affected by worldly thinking about homemaking? If so, in what ways?

6. What influence do homemakers have on their families, the church, and society?

Mother: Application

Tell your daughter some of the reasons you love being a homemaker.

Chapter Twenty-One

1. According to this chapter, what are three reasons for being prepared to be a homemaker?

2. Would you describe your heart as oriented toward home life? Why or why not? How can I encourage you to develop a heart for homemaking?

3. In what area of practical preparation for homemaking do you think you need the most help?

4. How does the priority of preparation for homemaking influence your plans for after high school?

5. Read the quote by John Angell James at the end of this chapter. What is one way I can help you understand your mission more thoroughly? What is one way I can help you prepare for your mission more diligently?

Mother and Daughter: Optional Activity

Sign up for a craft or cooking class together in your local community.

Chapter Twenty-Two

1. What was your favorite craft project in kindergarten?

2. What are good works, and what do they say about Jesus Christ?

3. Do you think that you resemble the woman devoted to good works? Why or why not?

4. Where should our good works begin? In what ways are you serving our family?

5. What, if anything, prevents you from being devoted to good works?

6. What are the good works that you think God has laid out for you? In the home? In the church? In the community?

7. By which of the young ladies' testimonies of good works were you most inspired? Why?

Daughter: Application

Ask your mom how you can excel at good works in the home. Then schedule an appointment with your dad, mom, and pastor to discuss serving in your church.

Chapter Twenty-Three

1. *What comes to mind when you hear the word* courtship? *Explain.*

2. *Would you say that God's Word shapes your outlook on courtship, love, and marriage? How so?*

3. *How does Jeremiah 29:11 encourage you regarding your future?*

4. *Are there certain qualities you've always wanted in a husband? How does God's criteria match up to your list?*

5. *Do you have thoughts, questions, or concerns related to courtship or marriage that you want to talk to me about? What are they?*

Mother and Daughter: Optional Application

Read a romance classic together and evaluate whether it expresses a godly or a worldly perspective of love, courtship, and marriage.

Chapter Twenty-Four

Mom, we're going to let you determine what is applicable to your daughter from this chapter.

Chapter Twenty-Five

1. *What was your favorite chapter from this book and why?*

2. Remind your daughter of her answer to your question back in chapter one: *"What is one way you hope our relationship will grow stronger and closer as a result of reading, discussing, and applying what's in this book?"* Has this happened?

3. *In what ways do you observe the attack on biblical womanhood in our culture and in the church?*

4. *What will be the effect when mothers and daughters display the qualities of biblical womanhood?*

5. *How can we be an example of biblical womanhood to those around us?*

6. *What is one way you want to help preserve the language of biblical womanhood for the next generation?*

Mother and Daughter: Optional Activity

Each write a letter to the little girl your daughter may have someday (her daughter, your granddaughter). Share with her the joys of your mother-daughter relationship and tell her of the importance of the language of biblical womanhood.

Appendix B
More GIRL TALK
Questions

For Mothers to Ask Daughters

1. Of which are you more aware: my affection and encouragement or my correction?

2. In what area(s) do you think I need to grow most?

3. Have you observed any area(s) in my life where my example doesn't back up my instruction to you?

4. How can I improve in the following areas?

Affection

Encouragement

Communication

Discipline

Friendship

5. Is there any way in which you think I have sinned against you?

6. Is there any topic you feel that we cannot discuss?

7. In what ways would you like to grow in your walk with the Lord?

8. What is your most difficult pressure or challenge at present?

9. Is there currently a pattern of sin in your life that discourages you?

10. Is there anything you need to tell me that you haven't already shared?

For Daughters to Ask Mothers

1. Do I actively pursue your guidance and counsel? How can I grow in this practice?

2. Do you feel that I value your wisdom more than that of my friends? Why or why not?

3. How would you characterize my attitude toward your authority?

4. What do you think I am most passionate about: my own selfish pursuits or serving in the home? Is there any way I can serve you at present?

5. How can I improve in the following areas?

Honor

Obedience

Gratefulness

Communication

Friendship

6. Is there any way in which you think I have sinned against you?

7. Do you think that my priorities—the way I spend my time—bring glory to God?

8. What skills can I cultivate to serve others and prepare for my future?

9. How have you seen me grow in my relationship with the Lord?

10. Is there anything you would like to discuss that I have neglected to ask?

Appendix C
How to Lead Your Daughter to Christ

We're mothers; so it goes without saying that we have a deep and strong love for our daughters. Their happiness and success are our joy, and their trials are our heartache. But nothing is more important than the state of our daughters' souls before God—not their schooling, hobbies, friends, or any earthly happiness. *Our ultimate mothering goal is that our daughters receive and reflect the gospel.*

No doubt this is your greatest desire and longing—that your daughter would come to a saving knowledge of Jesus Christ. This desire comes from God, honors God, and is the most genuine expression of love for your daughter.

Because a mother yearns for her daughter to know Christ, she may mistakenly pin her hopes on the slightest evidence of her daughter's salvation. She might choose to believe that her daughter's praying of the sinner's prayer as a young girl or her profession of faith today confirms that she is a Christian.

However, we must exercise discernment as mothers and avoid giving our daughters a premature assurance of their salvation. It is dangerous for them to assume that a confession or prayer alone is evidence of God's saving work. The Bible clearly states that we must repent and believe in order to be saved and that the fruit of a godly life will always accompany genuine faith.

Where authentic passion for God is displayed in a young

girl's life, along with consistent growth in holiness, there is reason to be encouraged. But if your daughter does not exhibit
hunger for God or hatred of sin, then you must share with her
your concerns. Do not promote a false sense of security regarding the state of her soul, but instead be faithful to remind her of
the good news of the gospel and urge her to repent and believe.

The following is a simple gospel presentation. It isn't a for-
mula for salvation, but rather a tool to help promote dialogue
between you and your daughter. In addition, I want to recommend *How Can I Be Sure I'm a Christian?* by Donald Whitney.
This book is an invaluable guide to the sometimes tricky questions of assurance.

While only the Holy Spirit can change your daughter's heart,
you can be faithful to pray for her and share the gospel with her.
May God reward your faithfulness and create new life in your
daughter's soul. He is "mighty to save" (Isa. 63:1).

How Good Are You?[1]

**How Would You Rate Your Goodness on a Scale from One
to Ten?**

If you're like most people, you probably gave yourself a six
or seven. You realize you're not as good as some people (you're
no Mother Teresa), but at least you've never murdered anyone.
God knows that you're a pretty good person, and because of this
He will accept you into heaven.

But is this true?

Did you know?

The Bible clearly teaches that we aren't good (Rom. 3:10-18).
Scripture also shows us that it's impossible to get to God by trying to be a good person or doing good works (Gal. 2:16). It's like
trying to jump from one end of the Grand Canyon to the other.
Some of us could jump farther than others, but none of us would
make it. We'd all fall short.

What's the standard?

The reason that most of us think we're good enough to get

to God is because we're comparing ourselves to other people instead of to God. We're using the wrong standard. Take a minute and compare yourself to God's standard (the Ten Commandments) to more accurately rate your goodness.

Check the laws you've broken.

1. You shall have no other gods before me.
Is God first in your life?
2. You shall not make for yourself an idol.
Are you devoted to anything more than God?
3. You shall not take God's name in vain.
4. Remember the Sabbath day, to keep it holy.
5. Honor your father and mother.
6. You shall not murder.
Hatred is considered murder (1 John 3:15).
7. You shall not commit adultery.
Lust is adultery of the heart (Matt. 5:28).
8. You shall not steal.
9. You shall not lie.
10. You shall not covet.

If getting to God depends on being good, we've got a serious problem! We'll take a closer look at this problem and God's amazing solution in the next three points.

1. Our Problem

We Are Sinful, and We Break God's Law. Sin Separates Us from God and Brings His Judgment.

We are sinful.

No one is good—not even one. . . . For all have sinned; all fall short of God's glorious standard. (Rom. 3:10, 23 NLT)

People were created by God to glorify Him and enjoy life in relationship with Him. However, each of us has turned against our Creator by violating His standard and living our own way (which is sin). God is perfectly holy. He is completely good and must respond in fierce opposition to our sin.

Sin brings judgment.

Because of your hard and impenitent heart you are storing up wrath for yourself on the day of wrath when God's righteous judgment will be revealed. (Rom. 2:5)

The final and irreversible punishment for those who die in their sins is eternal separation from God (2 Thess. 1:8-9).

2. God's Solution

Jesus Lived a Sinless Life. In Love Jesus Died as a Substitute for Our Sins.
God's love

For God so loved the world, that he gave his only Son, that whoever believes in him should not perish but have eternal life. (John 3:16)

Even though we turned against our Creator, He loved us and sent His Son, Jesus, to save us from His judgment. On the cross God the Son endured the holy wrath we deserve so that we could be forgiven and accepted by God.
Jesus' death

For Christ died for sins once for all, the righteous for the unrighteous, to bring you to God. (1 Peter 3:18 NIV)

Jesus did not remain dead. After three days Jesus rose to life and was seen by hundreds of eyewitnesses. Having conquered sin and death, He then returned to heaven as rightful ruler over all (1 Cor. 15:1-28).
It is not enough to simply know these truths.

3. Your Response

You Must Turn from Your Sins and Trust in Jesus Alone. Only Then Will You Be Forgiven and Accepted by God.
Turning from sin

Repent, then, and turn to God, so that your sins may be wiped out, that times of refreshing may come from the Lord. (Acts 3:19 NIV)

Trusting in Jesus

Whoever believes in the Son has eternal life; whoever does not obey the Son shall not see life, but the wrath of God remains on him. (John 3:36)

Think of it as like driving a car. Most people control their lives by deciding what they want to do and how they want to live. They are in the driver's seat. Those who trust in Jesus move out of the driver's seat and let Christ drive the car. They surrender control of their lives to Jesus' loving leadership.

You can trust Jesus right now.

Read over the prayer below to see if it expresses the desire of your heart. If it does, pray to God with faith, and He will save you.

"Lord Jesus, I believe that You died and rose again so that I could be forgiven and accepted by God. Please forgive me for breaking Your commandments. Today I turn from my sins and entrust my life into Your loving care."

For by grace you have been saved through faith. And this is not your own doing; it is the gift of God, not a result of works, so that no one may boast. (Eph. 2:8-9)

Appendix D
Mother-Daughter Memories

HERE ARE TWENTY-FIVE ideas to get you started making memories together:

1. Make reservations at a hotel or nice restaurant that serves afternoon tea.
2. Enroll in an art, cooking, or sewing class through your county or at a local retail store.
3. Take up a new sport (tennis, running, aerobics, biking, etc.).
4. Pamper yourselves. Get a facial or manicure and pedicure, or set up your own spa at home.
5. Do a service project (soup kitchen, nursing home, needy family, mom with young children, etc.).
6. Build a fire and roast marshmallows for S'mores. Play board or card games, or put a puzzle together.
7. Start a book club with some mother-daughter friends.
8. Go out for pizza and play miniature golf.
9. Do a cooking project. Bake bread or dessert, or prepare a full-course meal.
10. Get a makeover before a special event.
11. Pick fruit at a local farm and make something yummy.
12. Learn a new hobby, or spend an evening at a paint-your-own-pottery or scrapbook store.
13. Take a walk down memory lane. Watch home videos, look at family pictures, or dig up old family keepsakes. You can even use the Internet to learn what notable events occurred on the day you were born.

14. Schedule an annual mother-daughter overnight and pack it full of fun activities.
15. Do a progressive dinner and hit all your favorite restaurants in one night.
16. Take in some culture at a local art gallery or museum.
17. Go antiquing or shop at yard sales or consignment stores. See who can find the best deal.
18. Interview a relative about your family history.
19. Kidnap your daughter or your mom for a surprise outing.
20. Host a party for some mother-daughter friends. Do all the cooking and preparation together.
21. Collect decorating books or magazines and redecorate your room.
22. Pop some popcorn and watch an old movie together.
23. Have a picnic and read a book out loud, or take a drive in the country and listen to a book on tape.
24. Go to a local bookstore or coffee shop and share what you most appreciate about your daughter or mother.
25. And our personal favorite—have lunch and go shopping!

Appendix E
A Modesty Heart Check

*Women should adorn themselves in respectable apparel, with
modesty and self-control, not with braided hair and gold or
pearls or costly attire, but with what is proper for women who
profess godliness—with good works.*

1 TIMOTHY 2:9-10

Start with a Heart Check

❀ What statement do my clothes make about my heart?

❀ In choosing what clothes to wear today, whose attention
do I desire, and whose approval do I crave? Am I seeking to
please God or impress others?

❀ Is what I wear consistent with the biblical values of modesty, self-control, and respectable apparel, or does my dress
reveal an inordinate identification and fascination with sinful
cultural values?

❀ Who am I trying to identify with through my dress? Is the
Word of God my standard or is the latest fashion?

❀ Have I asked other godly individuals to evaluate my
wardrobe?

❀ Does my clothing reveal an allegiance to the gospel, or is
there any contradiction between my profession of faith and my
practice of godliness?

Before you leave the house, do a modesty check. (What are some
things you should look for as you stand in front of your mirror?)

From the Top

❀ When I am wearing a loose-fitting blouse or scoop neck,
can I see anything when I lean over? If so, I need to remember
to place my hand against my neckline when I bend down.

❀ If I am wearing a button-down top, I need to turn sideways and move around to see if there are any gaping holes that expose my chest. If there are, I've got to grab the sewing box and pin between the buttons.

❀ The same check is needed if I am wearing a sleeveless shirt. When I move around, can I see my bra? If I do, I need the pins again.

❀ Am I wearing a spaghetti-strap, halter, or sheer blouse? Not even pins will fix this problem! Most guys find these a hindrance in their struggle with lust. It's time to go back to the closet.

❀ Can I see the lace or seam of my bra through my shirt? In this case, seamless bras are a better option.

❀ More key questions: Does my shirt reveal any part of my cleavage? Does my midriff show when I raise my hands above my head? Is my shirt just plain too tight? If the answer to any of these questions is yes, then I need to change my outfit.

Moving on Down

❀ Does my midriff (or underwear) show when I bend over or lift my hands? If so, is it because my skirt or my pants are too low? Either my shirt needs to be longer, or I need to find a skirt or pants that sit higher.

❀ I also have to turn around to see if what I'm wearing is too tight around my backside or if the outline of my underwear shows. If so, I know what I have to do!

❀ And as for shorts—I can't just check them standing up. I need to see how much they reveal when I sit down. If I see too much leg, I need a longer pair.

❀ The sit-down check applies to my skirt or dress as well. And I must remember to keep my skirt pulled down and my knees together when I'm seated.

❀ And speaking of skirts, watch out for those slits! Do they reveal too much when I walk? Pins are also helpful here.

❀ Before I leave, I need to give my skirt a sunlight check. Is it see-through? If so, I need a slip.

❀ Finally I must remember to do this modesty check with my shoes on. High heels make my dress or skirt appear shorter.

❀ And don't forget—this applies to formal wear as well.

❀ A note on swimwear: It's not easy, but you can still strive to be modest at the pool or beach. Look for one-piece bathing suits that aren't cut high on the leg and don't have low necklines.

A Word to Fathers

by C. J. Mahaney

You may be a little uncomfortable right now. What rugged, masculine guy wouldn't feel slightly awkward holding a *pink* book entitled *Girl Talk*, much less reading it?

I can sympathize with your dilemma. After all, my name appears *inside* this pink book, written by my wife, Carolyn, and my oldest daughter, Nicole. And while it is not my general practice to contribute to a book of this color, I was honored when they asked me to make an exception in this case.

So if you are wondering what a book for mothers and daughters has to do with you, the answer is: everything. Why? Because *a mother-daughter relationship that is pleasing to God is dependent on the strategic and active leadership of the father.* That is why this masculine message in an otherwise feminine book has relevance for each of us.

As the father of not one, but *three* wonderful daughters (all of whom are grown and married and reflect their mother's godly character), I have been blessed with a very close and meaningful relationship with my girls. Nicole, Kristin, Janelle, and I share many happy memories of going to "the park with the swirly slide," playing Chutes and Ladders, and reading *Chronicles of Narnia* when they were little—going out for coffee, talking and laughing for hours, and reading *Deadline* when they were teenagers.

However, there were moments when I found my daughters a little hard to understand. I vividly recall several occasions when I thought I was gently instructing one of them only to have her burst into tears. I would seek out Carolyn's help: "I don't know what happened! One moment we were talking, and the next moment she was crying."

For fifteen years I was the lone male in our home before the birth of our son Chad. In other words, I lived with feminine mystery times four. But while I may not fully understand women, I do believe God's Word gives us clarity on how to father our daughters. Girls may be a mystery at times, but fathering daughters is not mysterious.

However, given the conflicting messages of our culture and the sin resident in our hearts, we are susceptible to numerous errors when it comes to fathering our daughters. Maybe you want your daughter to like you, and so you overindulge her every wish and lavish affection on her, while ignoring necessary discipline. On the other hand, you may be uncomfortable with your daughter's fluctuating emotions; so you remain detached and withdrawn. Or possibly you crave control, and as a result you are domineering and even angry at times. But none of these resemble a biblical approach to fathering.

Thankfully, Scripture plots a clear course for our paternal responsibility. And while I can't provide a comprehensive job description for fathers in these few paragraphs (any one point could fill a book), I hope this brief word will provide you with a God-glorifying plan for relating to your daughter.

The Bible clearly teaches that as a husband and father, I am the head of my wife and leader of my family. I am charged by God to serve and lead in my home (Eph. 5:23-33). This means that I am not to indulge, not to withdraw, and not to be harsh; I am called to exercise loving, gracious, and decisive leadership. All leadership must start with and proceed from an authentic godly example. But example alone is not sufficient. I am responsible to guide and direct my family in the ways of the Lord.

Now a key to being an effective father is being a godly husband. It may surprise you that I direct your attention to your marriage relationship, but the simple fact is that the most effective mothers are deeply loved wives. Women who are on the receiving end of passionate romance and tender care will be encouraged and equipped to fulfill their mothering task. To determine whether or not you excel in this area, why not ask your wife: "Do you feel more like a wife or a mother?" If she is more aware of her role as mother than as your wife, lover, and friend, then you may need to grow in expressing love, care, and romance in your marriage.

In addition to being godly husbands, we are called to be our daughters' spiritual leaders. God's Word has assigned us the task of bringing them up "in the discipline and instruction of the Lord" (Eph. 6:4). The Puritans understood this biblical principle. They considered each home a little church and every father the pastor of his family. So, as the resident theologians, we are responsible to teach our daughters the Word of God (Deut. 6:4-9). I'm not implying that your daughter needs to have a seminary education by the time she leaves your home. But I am appealing to you from Scripture that she needs to have a sound theological framework with the gospel at the center. (The classic book *Knowing God* by J. I. Packer would be a great place to start.) Because every verse of the Bible in some way reveals the person and work of Jesus Christ, all our biblical instruction must start with, continue in, and end at the gospel. Paul writes in 1 Corinthians 15:3 that the gospel is of "first importance." Therefore we need to be sure it informs and shapes our training.

Let me encourage you to set aside time during the week to instruct your daughter, care for her soul, and learn and grow together. These shouldn't simply be times of formal instruction but should also include the vital ingredient of friendship. One of many traditions my daughters and I enjoyed were regular father-daughter breakfasts where we discussed assigned reading from various theological books. Over Raisin Bran and cinnamon toast I endeavored to educate them about the glorious realities of the cross: justification, propitiation, and reconciliation, to name a few. Beyond reading assignments, I asked probing questions and engaged my daughters in theological discussions in an attempt to help them further grasp these gospel truths and apply them to their daily lives. And, of course, we had plenty of less serious conversations and riotous laughter as well.

In addition to teaching our daughters, we must spur them on in their passion for the Savior and for personal holiness. Aided by our wives, we must lead our daughters in the daily practice of the spiritual disciplines—reading God's Word, prayer, worship, service, and so on. By our own consistent example and instruction, we must help them understand the importance of regularly seeking God. Daily practice of the spiritual disciplines is an essential means that God has provided so we can grow in our knowledge of and love for the Savior. Therefore, the implications of our leadership in this part of our daughters' lives cannot be overstated. (I highly recommend to you Donald Whitney's book *Spiritual Disciplines for the Christian Life*. If your daughter is apathetic or deficient in her passion for God, or if you wonder whether or not she is converted, I encourage you, along with your wife, to read Appendix C on page 197.)

It is also vital that our gospel-centered teaching be intertwined with involvement in the local church. As fathers, we must passionately participate in the life of the church, wholeheartedly serve in the church, and graciously lead our family to do so as well. The church is at the center of God's plan on earth, and thus it should be central to our family life. I would also heartily recommend studying the doctrine of the church with your daughter. On this topic I know of no better resource than Joshua Harris's book *Stop Dating the Church!*

Men, I have barely scratched the surface of this serious and weighty responsibility to lead our daughters spiritually. But the God who has entrusted us with this task will also grant the grace and wisdom we need to fulfill it. As we look to our Savior, follow His Word, and rely on His grace, we can confidently expect His Spirit to graciously work in our daughters' lives.

I also want to strongly encourage you to lead your daughter into a close relationship with her mother. One of the greatest contributions you can make to your daughter's growth in godliness is to promote, facilitate, and encourage her friendship with her mother. God has assigned the task of training our daughters in biblical womanhood primarily to our wives. Titus 2:3-5 instructs the older women to "teach what is good and so train the young women." And what better woman to teach your daughter than her own mother?

I am sure you will agree with me: You and I are not equipped to educate our daughters on the finer points of biblical womanhood! However, by leading our daughters spiritually and theologically, we are laying the groundwork for our wives to "teach what is good"—to train our daughters in their understanding and everyday application of biblical womanhood. And Titus 2 is clear that when our daughters live out the qualities of biblical womanhood, they are actually putting the gospel on display (Titus 2:3-10). I can think of no higher incentive for promoting the mother-daughter relationship.

So consider: How much time do your wife and daughter spend together, one on one, building their friendship and discussing various aspects of biblical womanhood? If the answer is "not often" or "I can't remember the last time," then, Dad, your leadership and involvement is needed. In some cases, this may require you to look after younger children or arrange for a babysitter so your wife and daughter can have time together on a regular basis. In my case Chad was born when our daughters were in their early teens. So to enable my girls to be with Carolyn, I volunteered to watch Chad during the afternoon on my day off. I could think of no better way to spend these few hours than by being with my son and supporting Carolyn's relationship with our daughters. Also, if your wife or daughter participate in activities or carry responsibilities that prevent them from spending time together, help them to rearrange their schedule. Remember, the mother-daughter relationship is of vital importance to your daughter's spiritual growth.

Creating a context for our wives and daughters to develop a friendship is where we must start; however, promoting the mother-daughter relationship may require more intensive leadership on our part. For example, we are responsible to help our daughters fulfill the biblical mandate to honor and respect their parents, and in this case, their mothers. It is also of critical importance that we exhort and encourage our daughters to emulate their mothers' example. By communicating *our* respect, love, and admiration for our wives, we will provoke our daughters to follow in their footsteps. Finally, if there is a mother-daughter conflict, we are the designated peacemakers. And if you are unable to secure reconciliation between your wife and daughter, let me encourage you to request the involvement and assistance of godly friends and pastors. Remember, *a mother-daughter relationship that is pleasing to God is dependent on the strategic and active leadership of the father.*

I can tell you from experience that the rewards of fathering daughters far outweigh the labor of leadership that is required. It is impossible for me to describe the joy I experienced on the wedding days of each of my three girls. These events and all they include are forever etched in my memory. Perhaps most significant are the moments I spent with my daughters before I walked each of them down the aisle. There at the top of the aisle, as friends and family stood and watched and their soon-to-be husbands anxiously waited, I paused for one final teaching moment. It was an appropriate occasion to tell them that they could take this walk without regret—because of the way they glorified God and honored their mother and me. I drew their attention to the amazing grace of God that made this day possible. I thanked them for bringing me so much joy. And I told each daughter how grateful to God I was that she had become a godly woman like her mother.

So, Dads, let this be our vision and passion: to raise daughters who love the Savior, and through a close relationship with their mom, display the beauty of biblical womanhood.

Notes

Acknowledgments
1. Philip Doddridge, *The Rise and Progress of Religion in the Soul* (New York: The American Tract Society, 1745), www.ccel.org

Chapter 1: The Language of Biblical Womanhood
1. Edward Cody, "A Language by Women, for Women," *The Washington Post* (February 24, 2004): Sec. A.

Chapter 2: Imperfect Makes Perfect
1. "Declaration of Love," *Emma*, DVD, directed by Douglas McGrath (1996; Burbank, Calif.: Miramax Home Entertainment, 2003).

Chapter 3: Cover Mom
1. Donna Greene, *Growing Godly Women: A Christian Woman's Guide to Mentoring Teenage Girls* (Birmingham, Ala.: New Hope Publishers, 2002), 43.
2. Paul David Tripp, *Age of Opportunity: A Biblical Guide to Parenting Teens* (Phillipsburg, N.J.: P&R Publishing, 2001), 41.
3. Ibid.

Chapter 4: Afternoon Out
1. Paul David Tripp, *Age of Opportunity: A Biblical Guide to Parenting Teens* (Phillipsburg, N.J.: P&R Publishing, 2001), 80.
2. John Charles Ryle, *The Duties of Parents* (Conrad, Mont.: Triangle Press, 1888, repr. 1996), 35.
3. Susan Levine, "Staying Home for the Teen Years," *The Washington Post* (January 4, 2003): Sec. B.
4. Ibid.
5. Ibid.

Chapter 5: Constant Communication
1. Tedd Tripp, *Shepherding a Child's Heart* (Wapwallopen, Pa.: Shepherd Press, 1995), xix.
2. Charles Haddon Spurgeon, *Morning and Evening* (Peabody, Mass.: Hendrickson Publishers, 1995), 551.

Chapter 6: Conflict Jungle

1. John R.W. Stott, *The Message of Ephesians* (Downers Grove, Ill.: InterVarsity Press, 1979), 244.
2. Much of this chapter has been adapted from "Cravings and Conflict," an audio message by C. J. Mahaney, available at www.sovereigngraceministries.org.
3. David Powlison, *Seeing with New Eyes* (Phillipsburg, N.J.: P&R Publishing, 2003), 151.
4. David Powlison, "Anger, Part 1: Understanding Anger," *The Journal of Biblical Counseling*, Vol. 14, No. 1 (Fall 1995): 42.
5. Paul David Tripp, *Age of Opportunity: A Biblical Guide to Parenting Teens* (Phillipsburg, N.J.: P&R Publishing, 2001), 77.

Chapter 7: A Mother's Faith

1. Elisabeth Elliot, *The Shaping of a Christian Family* (Grand Rapids, Mich.: Fleming H. Revell, a division of Baker Book House, 1992), 180-181.
2. Tedd Tripp, *Shepherding a Child's Heart* (Wapwallopen, Pa.: Shepherd Press, 1995), 200.
3. Eric W. Hayden, *Highlights in the Life of Charles Haddon Spurgeon*, chapter 52 from the C. H. Spurgeon Collection, version 2.0 (Rio, Wis.: AGES Software, 2001), quoted in Steve Miller, *C. H. Spurgeon on Spiritual Leadership* (Chicago: Moody Publishers, 2003), 38.
4. Tripp, *Shepherding a Child's Heart*, 200.
5. Charles Haddon Spurgeon, *Morning and Evening* (Peabody, Mass.: Hendrickson Publishers, 1995), 128.

Chapter 8: A Mother's Example

1. Elisabeth Elliot, *The Shaping of a Christian Family* (Grand Rapids, Mich.: Fleming H. Revell a division of Baker Book House, 1992), 53.
2. John Charles Ryle, *The Duties of Parents* (Conrad, Mont.: Triangle Press, 1888 repr., 1996), 32.
3. Paul David Tripp, *Age of Opportunity: A Biblical Guide to Parenting Teens* (Phillipsburg, N.J.: P&R Publishing, 2001), 175-176.
4. John Angell James, *Female Piety: A Young Woman's Friend and Guide* (Morgan, Pa.: Soli Deo Gloria Publications, 1860, repr. 1995), 316.
5. Tripp, *Age of Opportunity*, 175.

Chapter 9: A Mother's Love

1. Erma Bombeck, *Motherhood: The Second Oldest Profession* (New York: McGraw-Hill Book Company, 1983), 5.
2. Ibid., 6.
3. John Charles Ryle, *The Duties of Parents* (Conrad, Mont.: Triangle Press, 1888 repr., 1996), 6.
4. Ibid., 4.

5. Paul David Tripp, *Age of Opportunity: A Biblical Guide to Parenting Teens* (Phillipsburg, N.J.: P&R Publishing, 2001), 73.

6. This list is adapted from my book *Feminine Appeal: Seven Virtues of a Godly Wife and Mother* (Wheaton, Ill.: Crossway Books, 2004), 128-132.

7. Charles Haddon Spurgeon, *Spurgeon at His Best* (Grand Rapids, Mich.: Baker Book House, 1991), 143.

8. Tedd Tripp, *Shepherding a Child's Heart* (Wapwallopen, Pa.: Shepherd Press, 1995), 195.

Chapter 10: A Mother's Discipline

1. John MacArthur, "A Crash Course in Christian Parenting," audio message (Sun Valley, Ca.: Word of Grace, 1997).

2. John Charles Ryle, *The Duties of Parents* (Conrad, Mont.: Triangle Press, 1888 repr., 1996), 7.

3. C. H. Spurgeon, *The Early Years, Autobiography,* Vol. 1 (Carlisle, Pa.: The Banner of Truth Trust, 1962), 43-44.

Chapter 11: A Daughter's Honor

1. Charles Bridges, *A Commentary on Proverbs* (Carlisle, Pa.: The Banner of Truth Trust, 1846, repr. 1998), 600.

2. Matthew Henry, *Matthew Henry's Commentary on the Whole Bible* (Montville, N.J.: Hendrickson Publishers, 1997), 125.

Chapter 12: A Daughter's Obedience

1. Paul David Tripp, *Age of Opportunity: A Biblical Guide to Parenting Teens* (Phillipsburg, N.J.: P&R Publishing, 2001), 76.

2. Tedd Tripp, *Shepherding a Child's Heart* (Wapwallopen, Pa.: Shepherd Press, 1995), 135.

3. John Piper, "A Vision of Biblical Complementarity: Manhood and Womanhood Defined According to the Bible," in *Recovering Biblical Manhood & Womanhood,* ed. John Piper and Wayne Grudem (Wheaton, Ill.: Crossway Books, 1991), 47.

Chapter 13: Sowing in Springtime

1. John Angell James, *Female Piety: A Young Woman's Friend and Guide* (Morgan, Pa.: Soli Deo Gloria Publications, 1860, repr. 1995), 35.

Chapter 14: It's a Girl!

1. Elisabeth Elliot, *Let Me Be a Woman* (Wheaton, Ill.: Tyndale House, 1987), 52.

2. Conversation with Jeff Purswell, October 15, 2004.

3. Ibid.

4. Ibid.

5. Ibid.

6. Wayne Grudem, "Men and Women: Similarities and Differences," audio message (Gaithersburg, Md.: Sovereign Grace Ministries, 2004).

Chapter 15: Foolish Fans and the Fear of God

1. Jerry Bridges, *The Joy of Fearing God* (Colorado Springs: WaterBrook Press, 1997), 10.

2. Ed Welch, *When People Are Big and God Is Small* (Phillipsburg, Pa.: P&R Publishing, 1997), 103.

Chapter 16: Best Friends

1. Charles Bridges, *A Commentary on Proverbs* (Carlisle, Pa.: Banner of Truth Trust, 1846, repr. 1998), 303.

2. J. C. Ryle, *Thoughts for Young Men* (Amityville, N.Y.: Calvary Press, 1996, 2000), 59.

Chapter 17: What About Guys?

1. Carolyn Mahaney, *Feminine Appeal* (Wheaton, Ill.: Crossway Books, 2004), 82.

2. Kris Lundgaard, *The Enemy Within* (Phillipsburg, N.J.: P&R Publishing, 1998), 24.

3. This chapter adapted in part from Mahaney, *Feminine Appeal*, 89-93.

4. Joshua Harris, *Not Even a Hint: Guarding Your Heart Against Lust* (Sisters, Ore.: Multnomah Publishers, 2003), 65.

Chapter 18: True Beauty

1. Interview with Jean Kilbourne by Susan Stamberg, "Beauty Series, Part 2: Pitching Beauty to Teens," NPR: *Morning Edition* Audio (June 22, 2004).

2. "Beauty Is a Curse: Halle Berry," (August 4, 2004) Rediff Entertainment Bureau, Rediff.com.

3. Quoted in ibid.

4. Matthew Henry, *The Quest for Meekness and Quietness of Spirit* (Morgan, Pa.: Soli Deo Gloria Publications, repr. 1996), 10-11.

5. Elisabeth Elliot, *Let Me Be a Woman* (Wheaton, Ill.: Tyndale House, 1976), 32.

Chapter 19: Taking God to the Gap

1. Quoted in Shannon and Joshua Harris, *Not Even a Hint: A Study Guide for Women* (Sisters, Ore.: Multnomah Publishers, 2004), 39.

2. Jason Perry, *You Are Not Your Own* (Nashville: Broadman & Holman Publishers, 2002), 109, quoted in Elizabeth George, *A Young Woman After God's Own Heart* (Eugene, Ore.: Harvest House Publishers, 2003), 194.

3. Quoted in Harris and Harris, *Not Even a Hint*, 39.

4. Perry, *You Are Not Your Own*, 109, quoted in George, *A Young Woman After God's Own Heart*, 194.

5. C. J. Mahaney, "The Soul of Modesty," audio message (from which this chapter has in part been adapted), available at www.sovereigngraceministries.org.

6. Ibid.

7. John MacArthur, *The MacArthur New Testament Commentaries, 1 Timothy* (Chicago: The Moody Bible Institute, 1995), 80-81.

8. Nancy Leigh DeMoss, *The Look: Does God Really Care What I Wear?* (Buchanan, Mich.: Revive Our Hearts, 2003), 26.

9. Quoted in Mahaney, "The Soul of Modesty."

10. Richard Baxter, *A Christian Directory*, in *The Practical Works of Richard Baxter*, Vol. 1 (London: George Virtue; reprint ed. Morgan, Pa.: Soli Deo Gloria Publications, 1990), 392, quoted in DeMoss, *The Look*, 20.

Chapter 20: Future Homemakers

1. John Angell James, *Female Piety: A Young Woman's Friend and Guide* (Morgan, Pa.: Soli Deo Gloria Publications, 1860, repr. 1995), 91-92.

2. Danielle Crittenden, *What Our Mothers Didn't Tell Us* (New York: Simon & Schuster, 1999), 22.

3. F. Carolyn Graglia, *Domestic Tranquility* (Dallas, Tex.: Spence Publishing, 1998), 92.

4. Carolyn Mahaney, *Feminine Appeal: Seven Virtues of a Godly Wife and Mother* (Wheaton, Ill.: Crossway Books, 2003), 103.

5. James, *Female Piety*, 72.

6. John MacArthur, Foreword to Pat Ennis and Lisa Tatlock, *Becoming a Woman Who Pleases God*, (Chicago: Moody Publishers, 2003), 12.

7. Dorothy Patterson, "The High Calling of Wife and Mother in Biblical Perspective," in *Recovering Biblical Manhood & Womanhood*, ed. John Piper and Wayne Grudem (Wheaton, Ill.: Crossway Books, 1991), 377.

8. Barbara Welter, "The Cult of True Womanhood: 1820-1860," *American Quarterly*, 18 (Summer 1966), 153, 174; quoted in Susan Hunt, *The True Woman* (Wheaton, Ill.: Crossway Books, 1997), 24.

Chapter 21: Homemaking Internship

1. Carolyn Mahaney, *Feminine Appeal: Seven Virtues of a Godly Wife and Mother* (Wheaton Ill.: Crossway Books, 2004), 21.

2. Lydia Maria Child, *The American Frugal Housewife* (Boston: Carter and Hendee, 1832), 96.

3. Tim Bayly, "Preparing for Motherhood: A Christian Response to the Cultural Attack on Domesticity," *Journal for Biblical Manhood and Womanhood*, Vol. 4, Nos. 2-3 (Winter 2000): 24-25.

4. John Angell James, *Female Piety: A Young Woman's Friend and Guide* (Morgan, Pa.: Soli Deo Gloria Publications, 1860; repr. 1995), 97.

Chapter 22: A Girl's Reputation

1. Jerry Bridges, *The Practice of Godliness* (Colorado Springs: NavPress, 1983), 232.
2. John R.W. Stott, *The Message of the Sermon on the Mount* (Downers Grove, Ill.: InterVarsity Press, 1978), 62.
3. Bridges, *Practice of Godliness*, 234.
4. Mark Dever, "The Importance of the Local Church," audio message (Gaithersburg, Md.: Sovereign Grace Ministries, 2002).

Chapter 23: When It Comes to Courtship

1. Elisabeth Elliot, *Keep a Quiet Heart* (Ann Arbor, Mich.: Servant Publications, 1995), 72.

Chapter 24: Who Gives This Woman?

1. Elisabeth Elliot, *The Shaping of a Christian Family* (Grand Rapids, Mich.: Fleming H. Revell, a division of Baker Book House, 1992), 186.

Chapter 25: Passing on the Language of Biblical Womanhood

1. Edward Cody, "A Language by Women for Women," *The Washington Post* (February 24, 2004): Sec. A.
2. Sara Groves, "Generations," from the CD *Conversations* (2001).

Appendix C: How to Lead Your Daughter to Christ

1. Adapted from the "How Good Are You?" tract © 2003 Covenant Fellowship Church. Used by permission. All rights reserved. To view the full-color tract with graphics or to purchase it online, visit www.howgoodareyou.com

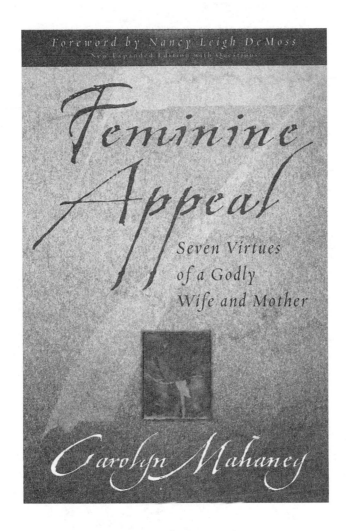

FEMININE APPEAL
New Expanded Edition with Study Questions

Carolyn Mahaney identifies with the challenges facing women in today's world and meets them with the guidance of God's Word. In this book of instruction for wives and mothers, she explores seven feminine virtues given in Titus 2 that have transformed her life and the lives of countless other women.